SENSUOUS
KNOWLEDGE

SENSUOUS KNOWLEDGE

A BLACK FEMINIST APPROACH FOR EVERYONE

MINNA SALAMI

AMISTAD

An Imprint of HarperCollinsPublishers

FIRST HARPERCOLLINS PAPERBACK EDITION PUBLISHED IN 2021

Designed by THE COSMIC LION

Library of Congress Cataloging-in-Publication Data is available upon request.

ISBN 978-0-06-287707-9

21 22 23 24 25 LSC 10 9 8 7 6 5 4 3 2 1

For my mother and father

Poetry is the place of transcendence.

—bell hooks

CONTENTS

SENSUOUS
KNOWLEDGE

INTRODUCTION
The Mountain

In a far and distant time, there was once an explorer who heard legends of a nearby mountain with natural riches so vast that it could make his town the wealthiest in the world. With his townspeople's encouragement, he took off to search for the mountain but returned months later with the disappointing news that although he found the mountain, it was arid.

Everyone forgot about the mountain eventually—all but one person who, led by a nagging feeling that there must be some truth to the legend, left the town in search of the great mountain. When this second explorer returned, she stunned everyone by reporting that the mountain was, after all, covered in lush vegetation, towering trees, and at least a few hundred species of plants.

In confusion, the townspeople began to incriminate one another. They accused the first explorer of plotting with neighboring towns. The second explorer's integrity was also called into question. However, both explorers were telling the truth; they had just viewed the mountain from different positions.

Working as a black, African-heritage woman in the white-and male-dominated world of ideas, I am like the second explorer who has navigated the other side of the metaphorical mountain. If the universal concepts—knowledge, power, beauty—in this book represent the mountain, I have written about them from the second explorer's perspective, in this case, an Africa-centered black feminist angle rather than the Eurocentric and patriarchal—what I shall refer to throughout the book as *Europatriarchal*—perspective from which we are accustomed to viewing them.

My primary motivation in writing from an Africa-centered black feminist perspective is, however, not to battle with the Europatriarchal view. It is not my aim to convince the first explorer that he's wrong about the mountain. That would place *him*, yet again, at the center of the narrative. What is important to me is the second explorer's *hidden* narrative, to put *her* world at the center.

I emphasize the word *hidden* because it is also not the point of *Sensuous Knowledge* to provide a "new" or "alternative" perspective to the Europatriarchal one. That would also center whiteness and maleness by implying that they are the axis around which everything else must turn. My blackness and femaleness are not "new" or "alternative" angles to me. They are the only angles that I know as far as race and gender are concerned.

Also, while blackness and womanhood are qualities that make me intrinsically understand oppression and prejudice, they do not automatically put me in the position of the victim, just as every white- and male-born person is not automatically an oppressor.

Ethnicity, gender, and race are chance factors that nonetheless, thanks to the narratives that shape society, greatly affect how we view the world and how the world views us.

I would not swap a comprehension of how reality is connected to these narratives for an illusion that I live in a color-blind, post-feminist, postracial, and meritocratic fantasy world. As the irreplaceable Toni Morrison once wrote when addressing the naivete that white women have historically been afforded by virtue of being looked after by women of other ethnic backgrounds, "Black women have always considered themselves superior to white women. Not racially superior, just superior in terms of their ability to function healthily in the world."

What she meant with these provocative words is that even if black womanhood can make life more challenging, to be a black woman is nevertheless a blessing, not least because it reduces the risk of a naive and ambivalent attitude to reality.

And so what is important about the explorer's hidden view is that it disrupts one-dimensional thinking and contributes to a more vibrant understanding of the world. Black feminists have always stressed that feminist discourses need to be anticapitalist and anti-imperialist, capitalism being a profit-centered system and imperialism the means through which the obsession with growth and profit is satisfied. There is no point in "smashing the patriarchy," as many Western feminisms claim to do, without fighting imperialism and capitalism. After all, there are no diamonds in European soil. There is no coltan in the USA. The resources that strengthen Western patriarchies are mostly unethically sourced from the Global South.

Fundamentally, patriarchal rule has also modeled systems of oppression on the violation of the environment. Developing a view of feminism as one in which humanity and nature live in a reciprocal relationship is a pressing task in the twenty-first century.

The Western feminist movement is, however, not monolithic, and *Sensuous Knowledge* draws inspiration from the international women's movement including figures such as the socialist revolutionary Rosa Luxemburg, ecofeminist Marie Mies, and the many Western activist groups from the Suffragettes to Women's Liberation to Me Too.

Although rooted in black feminism, *Sensuous Knowledge* speaks to the disaffected mood of the present time and is relevant to anyone who believes that the current Europatriarchal ruling systems are toxic and that we must develop paradigms of thought that instead are enlivening.

To rethink ideas that are central to the human mind with an Africa-centered black feminist sensibility is not to essentialize the ways that African, black, or female identities have been "othered" by a Europatriarchal value system. Instead, it is to unearth the subjectivity in these identities because, constructed as they may be, they shape our lives and so it is important to develop language and knowledge that works for and not against those excluded from the privileges of the status quo.

We may speak about knowledge as though it were a neutral term—as though the male perspective on beauty were the same as the female perspective. Or as though power could possibly mean the same thing to black people as a group as it does to white people as a group. And sure, knowledge itself is neither female nor male, black nor white. But because we typically interpret knowledge production with a white and male bias, women and men and people of different races and ethnicities relate to it differently. To quote Morrison again, "Narrative is one of the ways in which knowledge is organized."

The narrative through which we view knowledge is both the seed and the fruit of the culture it produces. To produce nourishing fruit, we need to plant sublime seeds.

And yet we typically try to cultivate a richer harvest with the same old weeds. We impose male norms on women's lives and the American Dream on every society. We raise girls so that they will grow up to become more like men but not boys to become more like women. We have to wonder why, despite all the feminist work, womanhood is still so devalued. Why do women still become annoyed when they are told (usually by men) that they are behaving like women? Conversely, why do they take pride in being told that they are behaving "like men"? Striving to become like men and adopt notions of masculinity is, frankly, setting a low bar. Men are just as enslaved by the social system—one that they hesitate to criticize because it amplifies an illusion about who they are. In fact, men are troubled with frustrated desires; they are caught up in the competitiveness of the rat race; they are sexually needy; they suffer from suicidal inclinations in disturbing numbers; and they possess an insatiable urge for power. Both women and men ought to reject the imprisoning definition of masculinity.

I'm not saying that men aren't privileged by these illusions of power. Precisely because of how power is defined, to be born male is to be born into a system that sees one's biological sex as superior to any other. But men are victims of what we can call the Superman syndrome, which is a cognitive dissonance that makes them erroneously believe that because the bars of their prison cell are golden, it is no longer a prison. The golden prison of masculinity sentences men to a life of conformity.

Nor am I suggesting that gender equality is not worth fighting for. But equality should not come at the cost of women's lived experience or what feminist philosopher Sandra Harding refers to as "socially situated knowledge," which means developing ways of looking at the world with women's lives and preoccupations at the center and where womanhood is consequently the norm.

There is no single "women's way of knowing," but one thing is for sure—knowing that is socially situated in womanhood is antipatriarchal. And so, obviously, grappling with the impact of dominance is unavoidable in writing about black-, female-, and Africa-centered worlds.

This grappling has not led to writer's block but to an equivalent sentiment that I refer to as writer's grievance. Writer's grievance is when you become starkly aware of the constant, howling objection in your words. It is when you wish that you could write about trivialities in the way that white male writers can. Or that you could be cool and impartial in writing about gender, as black male writers are. One cannot even single-mindedly write about a classic feminist issue such as the gender pay gap, as white feminists do, without that other issue spilling its *R*s and *A*s and *C*s and *E*s onto the pages.

Writer's grievance is similar to what the African American writer W. E. B. Du Bois referred to as "double consciousness" when speaking of racial issues in the United States. He wrote that double consciousness is "a sense of always looking at oneself through the eyes of others, of measuring one's soul by the tape of a world that looks on in amused contempt and pity." Because of institutional sexism and racism, so many of us come to look at the world in this way. We become a figure in the background of our lives, never really looking at the world with our point of view. Yet never placing myself (however constructed that self is) at the center of my worldview is the most harmful way for a black woman to live. I remain the "other" even to myself.

The result of such a displacement is that black women in the world of ideas feel like intruders. Entering conversations about the world's most significant discussions can feel like starting to watch a film halfway through. You may eventually piece together the plot, but you remain confused about the decisions the characters make. Why did the woman have an affair? Why did the cops blow up the building? Who the hell was that guy with the superpowers that appeared in the end? The truth is that many social conversations were not designed to be inclusive. As the brilliant and prodigious feminist writer bell hooks says, in a 2006 interview on the now-defunct Back Academics Platform, "Any woman who wishes to be an intellectual, to write nonfiction, to deal with theory, faces a lot of discrimination coming her way and perhaps even self-doubt because there aren't that many who've gone before you. And I think that the most powerful tool we can have is to be clear about our intent. To know what it is we want to do rather than going into institutions thinking that the institution is going to frame for us."

Hooks's quote points to why I didn't, however, suffer from writer's grievance while writing this book. My intention was clear: I did not want to write a protest book; I wanted to write a progress book. By *progress*, I refer to all three meanings of the word: first, something unfinished; second, onward movement; and third, raising consciousness higher.

The difference between protest and progress in this context is more subtle than it may first appear. However, there is one key distinction. Whereas a protest book would center on a fight to receive a leading role in the film—to continue the example above—a progress book is more interested in envisioning a movie that is inclusive and exciting from the very beginning. In essence, what principally motivated me to write this book was the desire to explore how concepts that shape what we perceive as knowledge change when you think about them with women's ways of knowing, black feminist theory, and African knowledge systems at the center.

In *Of Africa*, Nobel laureate Wole Soyinka wrote that Africa as we know it today "remains the monumental fiction of European creativity." But "if there is one offering that passively awaits to irradiate the world with a seminal humanism it is the 'invisible' religion in the African continent." The time to irradiate the world with the depth of insight from Africa's knowledge systems and the black diasporic culture derived from it is now. This insight has been devalued by a Europatriarchal worldview that has called it every possible name that would diminish it—primitive, tribal, urban, street, slang, third-world, you name it—for too long.

Women, by contrast, "see ourselves diminished or softened by the falsely benign accusations of childishness, of nonuniversality, of changeability, of sensuality," as the black feminist lesbian poet Audre Lorde wrote in *Sister Outsider*. We have been brainwashed to mistrust our ways of knowing that could be classified as feminine because the word *feminine* has been so abused. In her writing Lorde often referred to the "Black Mother" as an embodied feminine wisdom, a source of "that dark and true depth which understanding serves, waits upon, and makes accessible through language to ourselves and others."

African feminist knowledge systems imbue feminism with the knowledge of the metaphoric Black Mother. They bring in a love for spirit, as the author Alice Walker said in defining her influential theory, Womanism. Spirit means different things to different people. I use it to imply an individual and collective internal essence that makes our character, moods, beliefs, memories, and attitudes. To imbue knowledge with spirit is thus to view the arts, dance, proverbs, ritual texts, epic poems, musical traditions, creation myths, life histories, women's traditions, and utopias—all things you could say have to do with spirit—as sources of insight.

By interweaving the feminine and the masculine, the measurable and the immeasurable, nature and technology, history and futurism, the local and the global, the intimacy of poetry with the impassivity of science, the thrust of political reality with the tenderness of the arts, the innate knowledge of mythology and the critical thinking of intellectualism in an interdisciplinary fashion that draws from a range of traditions, ideologies, and streams of thought, I offer *Sensuous Knowledge* as a humble attempt to plant a seed that may blossom into what I hope is an invigorating

Africa-centered, woman-centered, and black feminist synthesis in the harvest of universal ideas.

When the second explorer returned from her visit to the mountain, her version of accounts excited the townspeople. Their eyes glinted with love when they spoke about this lush and bristling mountain. They became protective of the mountain as it became a part of their collective identity. Centuries later, when rises in carbon emissions threatened the mountain's flora, the townspeople did not hesitate to prioritize its preservation. Whatever divisions had cracked open between them were petty as they united in their commitment to rescue their beloved mountain. Because they had seen the mountain wholly, from all angles, they understood that discrepant views, however challenging, produced a richer understanding of the world.

The chapters that follow are portrayals from the other side of the mountain. As such, they are not meant to be definitive statements about the topics they address. Instead, they are intended to provide an investigation of ideas that, I hope, will inspire readers to reflect and formulate their own views.

We will begin our exploration by traveling from the old Yoruba civilization in Ife to Silicon Valley and back in search of a new interpretation of *knowledge*. We'll then explore *liberation* with the help of artists, mystics, and revolutionaries. We will steer toward shores of *decolonization* with oars made of ancestral feminist knowledge. We'll think of *identity* as a compass and as a commons. We'll welcome griots, scholars, and goddesses who travel from past epochs to tell us stories about *blackness* and *womanhood*. We will move around geographically, searching for the "blues" in the Futa Jallon Highlands, ancient Egypt, South Africa, and Yorubaland, and we'll return with new meaning for the feminist principle *"Sisterhood* is Powerful." We'll sail along three rivers—the Yangtze, the Thames, and the River Niger—to discover an empowering understanding of *power* and to learn how historical encounters along rivers have shaped power relations today. And we'll end our journey by cross-regionally and intergenerationally exploring the notion of *beauty*.

Yes, we will challenge Europatriarchal biases of knowledge, but not at the cost of spirit—that is, wonder, joy, embodiment, poesy, and play, or what we may call the sensuous.

of KNOWLEDGE

*To which poetry would be made subsequent, or, indeed,
rather precedent, as being less subtle and fine, but more
simple, sensuous, and passionate.*

—John Milton

*The true focus of revolutionary change is never merely the
oppressive situations which we seek to escape, but that piece
of the oppressor which is planted deep within each of us,
and which knows only the oppressors' tactics, the oppressors'
relationships.*

—Audre Lorde

In the beginning, there was only the sky, the sea, and the gods. Olokun was the Sea Goddess, and Olorun was the Sky God. One day, Obatala, the god of creativity, asked the Sky God if he could create land and living creatures to alleviate his boredom. Olorun approved, and Obatala created Ife, the great city that remains the cradle of Yoruba civilization. However, when Olokun found out that Obatala created earth and land in her territory without consulting her, she retaliated with a great flood that inundated the first city of humankind.

Eventually Ife was rebuilt, and it became the "*ondaiye* (the place of creation), *orirun* (the source of life), and *ibi oju ti nmo wa* (the place from where the sun, or enlightenment, rises)," as the eminent professor Banji Akintoye describes Ife in "A History of the Yoruba people." But the luminous strength of feminine wisdom was out of balance in the new Ife, and the genders were locked in an eternal power struggle.

To prosper, the people received *ogbon*, which refers to knowledge, or *phronesis* (practical wisdom). However, the gods knew that *ogbon* had to affect both the minds and hearts of the people. So they divided *ogbon* into *ogbon-ori* and *ogbon-inu*, concepts that literally translated mean "knowledge of the head" and "knowledge of the gut" but that respectively refer to intellectual intelligence and emotional intelligence. To have only one type of knowledge, according to the Yoruba epos, was to be only partly wise.

Just as *ogbon-ori* and *ogbon-inu* together form *ogbon*, so too are intellectual and emotional intelligence two sides of the same coin of knowledge. But throughout modern history, the dominant belief is that *all* worthy knowledge is rational and logical. The prevailing dogma is that all valid ways of knowing are strictly assessed by the cognitive skills of reasoning, quantification, and deductive inquiry. And so, from a young age, those with the best grades in subjects involving rationality and logic—mathematics, science, chemistry, and so forth—are graded the most intelligent. In fact, the mere tradition of ranking children is a result of this mode of thinking. As adults, we continue to evaluate intelligence according to ratable and hierarchical processes.

We do not view knowledge as something that can be accessed, and assessed, through the arts and their connection to the emotions, senses, and embodied experience. We associate talent with the arts but not knowledge. Yet art is also suited to explaining reality because art captures reality from the inside out. Art explains who we are because our existence is artful. We are not simply rational and mental beings, we are also emotional and physical beings. Art is a way to understand and change reality just as much as quanitifable information is. This is why *ogbon* had to speak to both the intellect and the emotions.

⋛∥⋛∥⋛∥∥

Stories turn into knowledge, and knowledge transforms into matter. The dualist worldview separates matter from story, but narrative *is* the matter from which we build our worldview, which in turn becomes physical objects: books, buildings, borders, and so on. In our bodies, knowledge also transforms into matter. Just as the first structure that forms in the human embryo is the spinal cord, so too is knowledge the spine of all other ideas that shape our lives. How we move and feel in the world, the air we breathe, the health of our trees, the food we eat, the ideologies we support, the way we dance and make love are all reflections of what we know.

The idea that calculable reasoning is the only worthy way to explain reality through is one of the most dangerous ideas ever proposed. Our approach to knowledge has become fundamentalistically rule-bound and rigid. Civilization thirsts for humanistic thinking as the Sahara is thirsty for water. The more robotic society becomes, the more social problems there are, which then once again encourages more surveyable diagnostics. As always, the poorest in society pay the highest price for this assessment-obsessed dynamic. In the UK, councils are increasingly using algorithms to make decisions about social welfare. Everywhere, rule-set, computable methods increasingly make key decisions about people's complex realities leaving those who most need to be listened to in the hands of a computer's authoritative verdict.

The incapacity to listen serves to suppress feeling, which results in toxicity because it overlooks actuality. The reason why the most violent people tend to be male is because the social education teaches men to repress their emotions. The repression of emotions always leads to violence, both physical and nonphysical—both toward oneself, and others.

We need an approach to knowledge that synthesizes the imaginative and rational, the quantifiable and immeasurable, the intellectual and the emotional. Without feeling, knowledge becomes stale; without reason, it becomes indelicate. We need an approach that measures wisdom not only by science, technology, engineering, and mathematics (STEM) or gross domestic product (GDP) but also by how ethically we develop our societies. We need knowledge that affects the interior as well as the exterior. *Ogbon-inu* and *ogbon ori*. Sensuous Knowledge.

By *sensuous*, I don't mean sensual. While sensuality is related to bodily appetites and self-indulgent pleasure involving the physical senses (touch, taste, sight, smell, and hearing), sensuousness transcends the instincts. When something is sensuous, it affects not only your senses but your entire being—your mind, body, and soul. Books are sensuous, for example. You can see, touch, and smell them. You can hear them in audio format and taste their words on your tongue. Books are tangible objects of myriad textures—aged, hardback, hand stitched and so on. They are mentally stimulating, therapeutic, and they potentially transform your deepest thought patterns. They affect you entirely.

When the poet John Milton coined the term *sensuous* in his 1644 tractate, "Of Education," it was precisely to avoid the sexual connotation in the word *sensual*. And so he described his genre—poetry—as one that was "simple, sensuous, and passionate." *Sensuous Knowledge* is thus a poetic approach; it is the marriage of emotional intelligence with intellectual skill. It is perceiving knowledge as a living and breathing entity rather than as a packaged product to passively consume. It is encountering knowledge as a partner rather than a servant—or as a lord, for that matter. It means treating knowledge as precious, so that it can hone you into an embodiment of its merit. Sensuous Knowledge is knowledge that infuses the mind and body with aliveness leaving its impact behind like the wake of perfume. It is knowledge that is pliable and not hard as rocks. Sensuous Knowledge means pursuing knowledge for elevation and progress rather than out of an appetite for power.

In the bestselling book *Thinking Fast and Slow* by Nobel Prize–winning neuropsychologist Daniel Kahneman, the author makes an argument similar to the ancient Yoruba philosophy of *ogbon*. Kahneman argues that we make decisions with the aid of two internal systems, which he calls system 1 and system 2.

System 1 is an emotional, intuitive system that "has little understanding of logic and statistics" while system 2 is a reflective, deductive system that is "capable of reasoning." You could say that system 1 is comparable to *ogbon-inu*, knowledge of the gut, while system 2 is comparable to *ogbon-ori*, knowledge of the head.

There is a crucial difference, however. In the typical binary way of Europatriarchal knowledge (if the names "system 1" and "system 2" don't already speak volumes), Kahneman sees the two systems as involved in "a psychodrama with two characters," with the emotional system 1 being the less intelligent character than the logical system 2. In contrast, you could say that the Yoruba mythological theory of knowledge sees the two systems in a passionate love story with two enamored characters instead.

I'm not presumptuous enough to dismiss the scientific research of a Nobel Prize–winning neuropsychologist, especially as I am not an expert on Dual Process Theory (DPT), the psychological field of which Kahneman's systems 1 and 2 are an example.

In fact, experts in the DPT field have challenged Kahneman's thinking. For example, in the provocative book titled *The Enigma of Reason: A New Theory of Human Understanding*, where researchers Hugo Mercier and Dan Sperber argue that the intellectual capacity to reason is itself an intuition—an emotional function. They argue that intuition, like reason, plays a huge role in our ability to make sense of our environment. The renowned neuroscientist Antonio Damasio has also put forward the idea that rather than being obstructed by emotion, as is usually assumed, reason is directed by it. According to Damasio's "somatic marker hypothesis," emotional experiences (or somatic markers) override reason when we make decisions. In short, our emotional response to a situation is the basis for our rational choice.

There are many other important, if conflicting, theories about the fundamental question in consciousness studies known as the mind-body problem. Epiphenomenalism posits that there is no such thing as the mind at all, that there is just a body reacting to life. Pantheism, at the other end of the spectrum, argues that the mind is a collective project of sorts where everyone is impacted by everyone else's thoughts and actions. As Baruch Spinoza, who is credited with forming pantheism, said in "Proposition Seven," "The order and connection of the thought is identical to the order and connection of things." But nobody has provided a satisfactory solution to what David Chalmers calls "the hard problem of consciousness," which simply put is the question of why humans have feelings. Perhaps, considering that we are only using half of our knowledge, *ogbon-ori*, it's no surprise that this remains a hard problem!

The truly hard problem is that the fragmented knowledge system in use today is unable to deal with the real issues confronting humanity because it neglects the experienced side of reality. Our educational systems are stale; they teach how to transform the brain but not the psyche; they explain how to design evolved societies but not how to be evolved citizens of them; they claim that emotions—central as they are to life—are incapable of explaining existence.

And so, despite living in the information age with an abundance of insight, we are incapable of solving pressing problems such as social injustice, sexism, racism, classism, speciesism, climate change, poverty, restlessness, mental health issues, and loneliness. Regardless of how educated or developed a society is, these same problems are causing despair and division everywhere. So we must concede that we are either approaching the wrong problems or we are approaching the problems wrongly. My stance is the latter. There is no soul to knowledge production.

The rigid, rule-bound, robotic way that dominates how we view knowledge today is what I refer to as *Europatriarchal Knowledge*, a hierararchy-fixated construct of knowledge that was initiated by elite European men as propaganda to solidify their worldviews on a massive scale.

The word *propaganda* comes from *to propagate*, which originally referred to the ability of plants to breed and multiply from one generation to another. It is etymologically apt, for the ability to adapt from generation to generation is precisely the magnificence of Europatriarchal Knowledge, the narrative that centers assessment and quantification as the epitome of knowing and that positions the European phenotype and male genotype as particularly gifted in the production of said knowledge.

Europatriarchal Knowledge has its roots in the Age of Discovery. It was during this period in history that European monarchs first sent explorers on voyages and expansions to world regions thought of as "the unknown."

They were motivated by an adage—"knowledge is power." It was the same saying that black progressives would later use as a slogan to end deception. However, whereas Civil Rights activists meant that knowledge is the power to determine "their destiny and identity," as *Ebony* magazine published in a 1969 special edition titled "The Black Revolution," the seventeenth-century British philosopher Francis Bacon, who coined the adage, meant it *literally*. Knowledge was a tool of control: it was man's God-given right to know and shape nature to his intents and purposes.

Bacon's *Novum Organon* (1620) helped to shift the general attitude in Europe away from the idea that knowledge was something to preserve, as it had been in medieval times, to the idea that knowledge was something to acquire, as it became in the modern world. It is typically Bacon's method of induction that is seen as a forerunner to the paradigm of knowledge we adhere to today, but I would argue that his contribution to perceiving knowledge as something we are in a race to acquire is just as crucial. *To acquire* means "to gain possession of," and this precisely is how we approach knowledge—as a quantifiable thing to be controlled and possessed in vast quantities, at all costs. Our politics, economics, laws, media, education, and policy are all formed around the fundamental position at the heart of Europatriarchal Knowledge, namely, that the purpose of amassing knowledge is ultimately to rank, compete, and dominate.

I use the phrase *Europatriarchal Knowledge* rather than, say, *empire*, *superpower*, or *white supremacist capitalist patriarchy*, as the black feminist scholar bell hooks astutely calls the system we live in, because in this book we are reimagining the narrative behind knowledge production (the framing story, or the metanarrative) rather than the structure it produces. The two are, of course, closely tied; the structural and political systems of white supremacy, capitalism, neoliberalism, and imperialism are the raison d'être of Europatriarchal Knowledge. The point of labeling it this way is, however, to distinguish the narrative from the structures that it creates so that we can, hopefully, explore if a different narrative would consequently produce a different structure. Basically, to change the structure, we first need to change the story about the structure.

It is possible. The Me Too movement, for example, has fundamentally changed the story of how we speak about sexual assault in the mainstream. It shifted the narrative from silence to voice, and from shame to blame. This in return changes structures in both the personal and political spheres by encouraging an emphasis on consent and the criminalisation of sexual abuse. There's a similar need to change the story in all oppressive social, economic and political contexts.

Also, while there's nothing positive to say about the *structures* of white supremacy, imperialism, elitism, and patriarchy, the *narrative* that produces Europatriarchal Knowledge is not altogether negative. The scientific, industrial, and information revolutions would not have taken place without a competitive race to acquire knowledge. In the absence of these revolutions, there would have been no (problematic) Enlightenment movement and, in turn, no encyclopedias, maps, trains, planes, modern universities, and many other institutions that in their own ways enhance our collective experience. Europatriarchal Knowledge has resulted in significant achievements, not least in the much-cherished development of rational thinking and reason. Rationality and reason are phenomena that we indeed should guard. To make it very clear, the point of Sensuous Knowledge is not to abandon induction or impartial judgment.

However, ironically, Europatriarchal Knowledge itself is not rooted in the rational objectivity it promotes. It is a constructed and biased narrative that brazenly centers whiteness and maleness. It is a narrative that parades propaganda as knowledge; it helps accumulate insight on how to end war, poverty, and disease yet doesn't end them. Instead of producing thriving, exciting, and wise societies, as knowledge should do, Europatriarchal Knowledge creates a world of social, political, psychological, and spiritual suffering. This is no accident. As long as there are social problems to solve, then more technical knowledge needs to be acquired—data, studies, surveys, analyses, expert panels, trade journals, you name it. The more resources that need to be pumped into technical knowledge, the stronger the idea that all knowledge is technical.

No matter all the erudition, Europatriarchal Knowledge will never come to grips with the problem of human suffering because ending human suffering would mean ending its rule. The algorithm is clear: so long as Europatriarchal Knowledge is the input, the output will favor the same pattern of thought. The only way to change the course of humanity is to challenge the input—to reimagine the way we think of knowledge with an altogether different, corrective story. A tabula rasa.

When you change the dominant narrative, everything changes along with it. That's exactly why there is so much propaganda to uphold it. Defeating Europatriarchal Knowledge is therefore a challenging process. It involves a completely new way of thinking and being in the world. It means seeing knowledge not as static but as a creative project, something that grows and advances—a human activity, an artwork. But that's precisely what makes it worthwhile.

To be clear, although sensuousness and sensuality are not synonymous I am not rejecting the erotic element. By contrast, you could say that I am arguing for an eroticization of knowledge. Europatriarchal Knowledge purges the erotic not least because of its association with the feminine. It dismisses the process of interweaving knowledge with the sensuous because it privileges the austere idea that knowledge may have nothing to do with embodied experience. In Europatriarchy everything is binary, *either/or*. It is either mind or body, either reason or emotion, either local or global, either nature or nurture, either feminine or masculine. But Sensuous Knowledge is kaleidoscopic, *with/within*. The mind exists with and within the body, reason with and within emotion, the feminine with and within the masculine, and vice versa.

Europatriarchal Knowledge also devalues the erotic, the feminine, and the poetic because they are connected to the natural world. What the Europatriarchal narrative essentially vilifies is interiority, *ogbon-inu*. Poetry is the language of the interior or the soul. Nature inhabits the interior of earth. And women's sexual organs, which carry *poiesis* (life, pleasure, and creation) are interior. Not only is the vagina a wet, warm, and dark place, like the enclave of a forest, it leads to an even more hidden yet life-bearing location, the womb. Surrounding all of this sexual interiority like an ozone layer is the clitoris, a poetic organ if ever there were one.

Humans are the only species that are distinctly poetic *and* erotic, and to degrade these qualities in knowledge production is to deprive knowledge of its humaneness and render it robotic. Poetry explains a feeling such as longing in the way the scientific method can't. Dance describes freedom in a way that mathematics cannot. Inner stillness explains existence in a way that technology can't. The acceptance of the raw, pure quality of interiority is essential to meaningful change. If we applied Sensuous Knowledge to the economy, for example, it would produce an "erotic economy" of sorts, in which reciprocity and sustenance rather than surplus and scarcity would thrive. If we applied it to education, children would take classes in subjects like empathy and dialogue as well as math and science. These topics would intermingle: in math class there would be a discussion of communication, and in empathy class, statistical patterns as well as artworks would be analyzed.

A verse from a poem by a Chinese poet from the Jin dynasty (CE 266–420), Zi Ye, or "Lady Midnight," shows how the boundary between knowledge, poetry and eroticism can be blurry:

> *All night I could not sleep*
> *Because of the moonlight on my bed.*
> *I kept on hearing a voice calling:*
> *Out of Nowhere, Nothing answered, "yes."*

The "yes" in the poem could correspond to a natural desire to know an answer to a question, perhaps a spiritual query. It could also connote a "yes" to the touch of a lover. The moonlight evokes both clarity and mystery, and the sleepless nights may be caused either by passion or deep thought. When the "yes" emerges, it appears simultaneously enlightening and erotic. But we can also sense the anxiousness that the poet feels about this "yes." When you are socialized to think "no," then "yes" comes out of "nothing and nowhere," startling you like a ghost. Or as Audre Lorde said, "We have been raised to fear the yes within ourselves."

Lorde argued in her essay "The Uses of the Erotic" that the erotic is a resource "that lies in a deeply feminine and spiritual plane." Its suppression is the suppression of "a considered source of power and information within our lives," she wrote. In another essay, "Poetry Is Not a Luxury," Lorde argued that poetry is a "vital necessity" for women's existence because it is through poetry that we fashion a "language that does not yet exist." The fusion of what Lorde referred to as the "European mode" of knowing— what I refer to as Europatriarchal Knowledge—which centers on problems and solutions, with the "Non-European consciousness," which focuses on interactivity with real life, was, she wrote, "necessary for survival" and is, in Lorde's view, best derived through poetry. To think of poetry as a luxury is thus to discard "what we need to dream." It is to neglect precisely what we need "to move our spirits most deeply and directly toward and through promise." It is, in essence, to claim that our very "womanness" is a luxury.

One of the earliest poems ever written anonymously in ancient Egypt, ca. 2000–1100 BCE, also illustrates the closeness of knowledge and Eros:

Your love has penetrated all within me
Like honey plunged into water,
Like an odor which penetrates spices,
As when one mixes juice in

The poet is likely to be speaking of the delight ("honey plunged into water") of a transformation caused by a spiritually inclined epiphany, but the language evokes lovemaking. The French-Moroccan philosopher Alain Badiou says in "In Praise of Love" that love is cultivated not solely by the mind but "through a transcendent force." In this poem, the transcendent force could equally be a lover or knowledge.

Those who seek to destroy progress—fundamentalists, imperialists, sexists, corrupt governments, white supremacists, military men, greedy corporations, and so on—discourage a sensuous approach to knowledge because tyrants have always understood that the more robotic people are, the more easily manipulated they are. This is why colonizers confiscated indigenous art. It is why organized religions destroyed evidence of goddess worship; it is why the Taliban blew up the ancient art of Afghanistan. It is the reason fundamentalists burned libraries in Timbuktu. It's what caused Hitler to ban anti-Nazi art and literature in Germany and it's why the Turkish military has destroyed Kurdish monuments. These violent autocrats know that the more you prevent an experience of knowledge as living and evolving, the higher the chances of upholding power. They understand that a mind that is frightened, fragmented, and frustrated is the least likely to resist oppression and the most likely to perpetuate it. Those who wish to maintain the status quo will do everything possible to prevent the transformation of knowledge. They know that a person who cannot think for themselves is a person who can think for *them*.

≡⫴≡⫴≡⫴

If there is a group that always has challenged the premise of Europatriarchal Knowledge, it is black feminists. Due to our position outside the center of power with respect to race, gender, and often class, black feminism provides not the only but the most rounded critique against Europatriarchal Knowledge. Black feminists have always emphasized that the struggle cannot be against only patriarchy, as white feminists have said. Neither can it push back against only class, as socialists have said. It cannot tackle only race and imperialism, as black radicals have said. And it cannot only tackle ecocide, as environmental campaigners have said.

This is why black feminism offers a relevant countercultural approach against the knowledge system that governs our world for everyone. There is no other ideology—not socialism, not Marxism, not black radicalism or white Western feminism—that at core has created liberation theories for addressing class, gender, and racial discrimination combined. While the black liberation movement has made important contributions toward ending imperialism, and while white feminists have made strides toward the dissolution of patriarchy, and while socialists have critically addressed class, it is only in black (and WoC) feminism that we consistently find a resistance to all of these oppressions which growing numbers of people increasingly realize are connected.

As is written in the classic black feminist statement The Combahee River Collective Statement, "If Black women were free, it would mean that everyone else would have to be free since our freedom would necessitate the destruction of all the systems of oppression."

Black feminists also always integrally understood that we need new ways of conceptualizing what we *know*. Again and again, black feminists have argued that because the reigning system is a soulless one, the remedy is a way of knowing that incorporates poetry and art, the language of love.

Consequently, black feminists argue that creative expression is a vital form of knowledge production because it aids the development of emotional intelligence. For a group historically denied access to education, black women have survived by relying on the in-depth, intuitive, and poetic knowledge of creative expression not only for entertainment but also for critical insight.

For instance, in her song "Beware, Verwoerd," Miriam Makeba hid an antiapartheid message in the chorus that urged black people to resist apartheid by instead warning the white military man, "Verwoerd," of black insurgency—a line that later became a protest slogan. In "Four Women," Nina Simone pronounced the names "Aunt Sarah," "Saffronia," "Sweet Thing," and "Peaches" with emphasis—to intervene against a culture that erases and silences black women. Each of these is black feminist knowledge production.

When Beyoncé, in her album *Lemonade*, pontificated that she was no "average bitch" and that if her lover neglected to value her she would soon be gone to the "next dick" it was a black feminist message that women should not accept bad behavior from men.

In 1897, when Zanzibar abolished slavery, previously enslaved women began a fashion they called *kanga*. They sewed together the handkerchiefs that were brought by Portuguese traders sailing into Zanzibar harbors and used them to express their freedom. This knowledge practice helped toward mending historical divisions not only between slave and free but also between Arabs and Black Africans and between women and men.

Black feminist theories such as the sociologist Patricia Hill Collins's "ethics of caring" expound on this insight. According to Hill Collins, the psychological effect of sharing the impacts of classism, sexism, and racism mark black and African women's lives around the world with a unique tendency that she refers to as an ethics of caring. Founded upon three pillars, the ethics of caring includes: first, the value placed on individual expression; second, the value of emotions; and third, the capacity for empathy. Hill Collins argues that African humanist and feminist principles influence black women's ways of knowing. Access to both Afrocentric and feminist standpoints distinguishes black feminism from white feminism not because the latter does not emphasize women's creative expression but because it doesn't validate it as a way of knowing.

Or think of Alice Walker's "In Search of Our Mothers' Gardens," the essay in which a garden becomes a symbol for knowledge production. According to Walker, because black women were historically forced to bear the "burdens that everyone else—*everyone* else—refused to carry," they were unable to record knowledge. Walker argues that they consequently transmitted knowledge through creativity—making quilts, telling stories, and nurturing gardens. Writing about her own mother's garden, Walker says, "Whatever shabby house we were forced to live in . . . she turned into a garden so brilliant with colors, so original in its design, so magnificent with life and creativity." These expressions, she argues, were how black mothers historically and intuitively knew how to teach their daughters about freedoms they themselves had not been fortunate enough to enjoy.

Bell hooks argues in her essay *"Theory as Liberatory Practice"* that theoretical "work by women of color and marginalized groups of white women (for example, lesbians, sex radicals)" is the most liberating type of academic knowledge because it interweaves the personal. In her typical clear, compassionate style influenced by a Christian upbringing and Buddhist practice, she adds in her book *Teaching to Transgress* that creative work crafted "from the location of pain and struggle . . . is often de-legitimized in academic settings" despite being the exact type of insight that can set people free.

Toni Morrison, in her 1993 Nobel Lecture, told the story of a group of youngsters trying to expose an old, blind, clairvoyant

woman as a fraud. "Old woman," they said, "I hold in my hand a
bird. Tell me whether it is living or dead." The woman remained
silent for a long time, causing the youngsters to laugh cockily.
Then suddenly she said, "I don't know whether the bird you are
holding is dead or alive, but what I do know is that it is in your
hands. It is in your hands." If the bird represents a narrative, then
the old woman's message is that it ultimately does not matter what
the story is right at this moment. What matters is that it's in the
youths' hands to tell it. "Oppressive language does more than represent violence; it is violence; does more than represent the limits
of knowledge; it limits knowledge," Morrison continued. "Sexist language, racist language, theistic language—all are typical
of the policing languages of mastery, and cannot, do not permit
new knowledge or encourage the mutual exchange of ideas." In
short, Morrison argued, as I am, that our perception of knowledge
shapes our reality.

The novelist and feminist Chimamanda Ngozi Adichie expresses a similar message in her TED talk, "The Danger of a Single Story." "There is a word," she says, "an Igbo word, that I think
about whenever I think about the power structures of the world,
and it is *nkali*. It's a noun that loosely translates to 'to be greater
than another.' Like our economic and political worlds," Adichie
argues, "stories too are defined by the principle of *nkali*: How they
are told, who tells them, when they're told, how many stories are
told, are really dependent on power."

≣∥≣∥≣∥

I conceived of the phrase "Sensuous Knowledge" during a visit
to the Singularity University at NASA's Ames Research Center
in Silicon Valley to give a talk. It was during daily swims in the
camp's pool that the phrase appeared. I love swimming generally,

but diving into this pool was like ensconcing myself in a soft, blue velvet blanket. Later I understood that the pool symbolically represented interiority to me, both because of its location at the center of the research camp and because it felt like the safe harbor of a womb.

At the time, I was working on a project titled "Big Ideas Change the World" for the environmental charity Friends of the Earth. I was interested in connecting feminist theory with ideas about technology, global governance, and climate engineering, and the Singularity University was an exciting place to strengthen my critical arguments.

The keynote at the event was Ray Kurzweil, the futurist who coined the notion of the singularity—a hypothesis that machine and human will converge in the future. Everyone, including me, anticipated Kurzweil's talk. I expected it to enrich my research. I was not mistaken; his presentation was fascinating and insightful. He was surprisingly humble and soft-spoken, which I found refreshing after a day of talks presented in the typical American, masculine way of pompously striding around the stage.

Several conversations that week stimulated and touched me in this way. I'd expected to spend the week with robotic tech-bros and Silicon Valley fanatics. Instead, I found myself in the company of people who mostly were genuinely passionate about ideas that could make a difference. We spoke about the big four technologies of the future—nanotechnology, biotechnology, information technology, and cognitive science (the NBICs). We thought about the intersections between tech and consciousness, and we watched a sensational clip of a little girl controlling a toy car with her mind. In between the discussions, there were yoga classes and wholesome meals. In short, the trip was rewarding.

But the visit also provided an unnerving glimpse into a future that could be utopian—one where health care, poverty, social inequality, and climate change were solved—but one that our current mind-set would never manifest.

I recall a chilling conversation with a group of people, all wealthy, white and male, who in all seriousness expected to live at least into their midhundreds thanks to life extension technology (reverse aging, epigenetic rejuvenation, antiaging supplements, and so forth). They were roughly my age, yet they spoke with the certainty that they would live another century. I failed to mask the horror I felt when these people, who were privileged in race as well as class, talked excitedly about their futures. It was not a future that I or most of the planet's people can even dream of.

I did not have moral qualms about life extension technology itself. I'm not against exploring how science can improve and extend life. I am against developing new technologies mindlessly in the wrong direction. I'm against people being encouraged to behave as though they live on an isolated island where their decisions don't affect others. I'm against the unfathomable inequality between those who are lucky if they live a handful of decades while others are already planning to live well into their second century. I'm against the increasingly cozy relationship between scientific research and profit-driven corporations that have the ability to control so many aspects of people's lives. It is no coincidence that some of the key investors in life extension are the founders of corporations such as Google, PayPal, and AstraZeneca.

Science is of course the most reliable way of validating hypotheses. But science has also been used to justify crimes from the transatlantic slave trade to the Holocaust to the exclusion of women from public life. The scientific world is still full of racists and sexists using "science" to validate their prejudices. Hardly a month passes without some new scandal related to the misuse of the scientific method. I'm reminded, for example, of Satoshi Kanazawa, evolutionary biologist at the London School of Economics, who in 2011 published a "scientific" article in which he argued that "Black women are less attractive than other women." A surreal feeling creeps to the surface when I think that the reputable platform *Psychology Today* published those offensive words on its blog. What troubles me mainly, however, is not Kanazawa's racism, which is transparent and trite, but rather that his words could still be taken seriously in our times. As anthropologist Jonathan Marks writes in his polemic *Is Science Racist?* "To suggest that a scientific study of race can somehow shield or immunize itself from culture or politics is itself a highly political dissimulation."

To argue that scientific output should be received with the same critical lens as one might engage with, say, literary criticism or art criticism, is to run the risk of being called antiscientific and anti-intellectual. Science is the religion of modern Europatriarchy, and like all faiths it imagines itself to be beyond question. There are repercussions for questioning an inherent neutrality in scientific knowledge production. To do so as a black woman—and in a chapter about knowledge—is to invite accusations of being uninformed, or worse. And yes, I am aware of my limited insight into the academic debates about epistemology, the study of knowledge. Such conversations are held in an abstract language with which neither I nor, I imagine, most of my readers are comfortably familiar. However, I can say with confidence that, with the exception of feminist and postcolonial studies, which have radically impacted knowledge production, the debate still predominantly invokes Enlightenment-era philosophers who established the Europatriarchal Knowledge narrative by encoding their biases into the field of science. The world is suffering because of the biases in knowledge. But the even deeper reason for inequality is that our conceptualization of knowledge only permits bias as a way of relating to it.

Also, my visit to the NASA Research Center was far from the only time that I've lost sleep over the lack of thoughtfulness, empathy, and sensitivity about the future of humanity. All my work stems from despair caused by the oppression of women and the subsequent discrediting of qualities deemed to be feminine such as the above despite how essential they are to successful education, politics, culture, business, social relations, and science.

But the experience prompted the urgency of addressing Europatriarchal bias in scientific knowledge especially as new technologies replicate the same models of thinking. I do not mean only the way it is gendered, racialized, classed, and so forth. But what moral and ethical questions underpin the scientific method? What is the worldview that brought us to present-day society? And how can we change it? For if knowledge production is unethical today, then the knowledge produced will be unethical in the future too.

That science can uphold its overarching reputation as inherently objective despite critical evidence to the contrary goes back to the perception of knowledge as an acquisition shaped by early Europatriarchs such as Francis Bacon. Few people question this particular element of biased knowledge production but it is the root that sustains the status quo. For when you think of knowledge as an acquisition, you must first think of it as res extensa, something separate from you. After all, you cannot acquire what you already own. This distinction, in turn, requires that you perceive knowledge as something that manifests of its own accord, which means that you must see knowledge as neutral. Conversely, to view knowledge as neutral, you have to separate it from the thought patterns and social conditions that created it. To sustain the belief in this process, you must propagate that the most valid form of knowledge is that which can be measured. Ultimately, this is how the process of Europatriarchal Knowledge works. Acquiring knowledge at any price distances it from context and promotes bias.

≡⫴≡⫴≡⫴

When I was six years old, Audre Lorde published her widely read essay "The Master's Tools Will Never Dismantle the Master's House." I didn't read it until much later, of course, at a point when I had left a career in marketing and launched a feminist blog titled *MsAfropolitan* that was growing fast. I planned to do a master's in gender studies so that I could give my writing the insight that sharp commentary requires. I chose the School of Oriental and African Studies, where I could focus on black and African feminist perspectives on gender. In preparation, I read many nonfiction books by black feminists, including Lorde's *Sister Outsider*, which touched my core. When she said, "The master's tools will never dismantle the master's house," it was as though she spoke directly to me. I wanted to ask her, "Then *which* tools will?"

I was not alone in agonizing over this question. Since its publication in 1984, many people have asked which exact tools Lorde referred to. In op-eds, essays, workshops, dissertations, protest slogans, panels—you name it—everyone asks the question: Which tools? Everyone vested in the liberation of women, of nonwhites, of the poor, of indigenous people, of the environment, everyone involved in countercultural thought, yearns to identify the master's tools.

Most analysts argue that the master's tools are systems such as capitalism, colonialism, or Enlightenment thought. A study I came across argued convincingly that legislation governing plant seeds is a master's tool. Others advocate (more conservatively) that the master's tools are devices such as craftiness, strategy, and deviousness. To such interlocutors, "a tool is a tool," and what better way to demolish the master's house than with his own devices?

The discussions are endless, but they miss a crucial element. To determine what tools to discard, we need to focus on the object they built—the master's *house*. There is so much emphasis on the word *tools* that we have missed the significance of the word *house*.

If we shift our focus to the metaphorical master's house, we will see that it is a bluff. It's a prison designed to look like a home, a dungeon camouflaging as a palace, a sad place pretending to be a happy place. Even the word *house* as we understand it today is not as a place of coziness and warmth but a place of market value, privatization, and ego extension.

You can hang decorations in the master's house. You can spray slogans about freedom on its walls. You can create altars of equality in its gardens. But the master's house will still be a prison for everyone but the master himself. What price do we have to pay for staying in the metaphorical master's house? Why fight for a seat at its tables? Why uncritically celebrate blackface positions in imperialist structures or "woman-face" patriarchs? The only way to be free is to get out of the master's house.

The point here is not to go live with the fairies in the woods but, instead, to understand that to *dismantle* means to "remove the mantle." To see through the illusion of the master's house is to remove the mantle or, if you like, to "dis-mantle" it because it is only when we see reality clearly that we can change it. Sensuous

Knowledge is about seeing reality clearly, wholly, with all our faculties.

As for the master's tools, here's what they are not: the master's tools are not poetry, playfulness, Eros, borderlessness, conscientiousness, dialogue, intuition, soulfulness, stillness, warmth, passion, beauty, compassion, mystery, wisdom, honesty, femininity, interiority, sensuousness, *ogbon-inu*.

≡ⅶ≡ⅶ≡ⅶ

African knowledge systems have long provided a treasure trove of narrative for informing feminist ideas of knowledge. With the oldest civilizations in the world, Africa also has some of the oldest patriarchies, and so it is in the African continent that we find some of the oldest protofeminist narratives.

Women in traditional African society were not domesticated wives. They were traders, politicians, farmers, artists, and shamans. They were goddesses, witches, prophetesses, queen mothers, rain queens, pharaohs, and spirit mediums.

In African creation myths, there is no overarching supreme male god. If anything, there are traces of history that suggest that all Africans once worshipped a mother-goddess. That is not to say that there is always gender harmony among the pantheon of deities. Hardly! The gods get into kerfuffles concerning gender, as humans do, precisely so that they can show what happens when we don't at least strive for harmony.

Moreover, the underpinning myths are egalitarian with respect to nature and species. The Yoruba gods, like many of their counterparts in other African religious systems (the earth goddess Asase Yaa in Ghana, Dzivaguru in Zimbabwe, Mamlambo in South Africa), are anthropomorphic representations of nature elements. A person invested in African spiritualities, therefore, treats nature with compassion. Similarly, animals are not viewed as inferior to humans because we all depend on life in an equal manner. Animals in African myths are companions who can even occasionally marry humans and produce children who are both human and animal. Animals are also teachers, each with a specific lesson to teach. The tortoise, for example, shows how to watch out for dishonest and mischievous behavior by itself being guilty of that. Anansi the Spider in the eponymous Ghanaian tale similarly teaches about mischief by getting into mischief. It is not only in myths that Africans cohabit with animals. The Maasai people, who very rarely eat meat, have lived together with wildlife—giraffes, zebras, lions, leopards, and hyenas—for centuries and are not afraid of them. Unlike Europatriarchal Knowledge, historical African knowledge systems—like other indigenous ones—emphasize the value of harmony not only with other humans but also with nature and other sentient beings. African philosophy is a philosophy of interbeing.

Unlike some organized religions, African spiritual philosophies have no heaven or hell because, at large, they do not believe that there is such a thing as death. The souls of the departed are not punished for their sins in hell by a Manichean devil. In African spiritualities, the dead are supposed to "live" in transmigrated form or on nonphysical planes of the cosmos. According to Yoruba culture, the human spirit is triple layered—force or breath, shadow, and spirit (*emi, ojiji,* and *ori*). The Zulu have a similar triad—*idlozi* (guardian spirit), *umoya* (breath), and *isithunzi* (shadow)—and to the Igbo the human spirit is made up of *uwa* (visible world) and *ani mmo* (spiritual world). To ancient Egyptians, *ba, ka,* and *akh* were components of the soul that respectively represented the life force, the spirit force, and the unity of the two, which transcended this world and reached into the next. As a consequence, knowledge is not something that one must acquire and hoard during life, for wisdom and existence are infinite and eternal.

Significantly, African philosophies encourage creative expression (art, dance, ritual, sculpture, and so forth) as the highest form of knowledge. Ritual is reflective not only of spirituality but also of knowledge sharing. Deities are not simply divine energies, they are also representations of philosophy. Each god is a literation of a concept. For example, Shango, the spiritual embodiment of thunder, is also a historical reading of an African philosophy of social justice. Oya, goddess of tornadoes and protector of women, provides an interpretation of feminism in ancient Africa.

In her last book, *Socrates and Orunmila: Two Patron Saints of Classical Philosophy* (2014), the late Nigerian feminist philosopher Professor Sophie Bosede Oluwole offered a groundbreaking comparison between Socrates, the founder of Western philosophy, and Orunmila, the author of the Yoruba compendium of knowledge known as Ifa. The corpus of Ifa, which now also exists widely in written format, is a geomantic system consisting of 256 figures to which thousands of verses are attached. It has been stored through memory for millennia by traditional Yoruba philosophers known as *Mamalawos* and *Babalawos* (mothers and fathers of esoteric knowledge, respectively), who must study Ifa for fourteen years before being allowed to share its wisdom.

Oluwole wondered why Socrates, who did not produce any written work, can be considered the father of Western philosophy when Orunmila, who also transmitted his ideas to his disciples without writing them down, could not. Where Socrates famously said, "An unexamined life is not worth living," Orunmila said, "A proverb is a conceptual tool of analysis." Where Socrates said, "The highest truth is that which is eternal and unchangeable," Orunmila noted, "Truth is the word that can never be corrupted."

Where Socrates said, "Only God is wise," Orunmila too addressed the limits of human knowledge in his statement "No knowledge-able person knows the number of sands." Oluwole urged Africans to reclaim their philosophical heritage, contending that the body of knowledge she found in the Yoruba tradition was as rich and complex as any found in the West.

I take a critical view of elements of African spiritual life as I do of all other forms of religion. I am especially critical of the pa-triarchal, authoritarian, and gerontocratic (rule by elders) way of thinking in many African philosophical histories. Even if women in ancient Africa had spiritual power, misogyny was not imported from Europeans. Misogyny as we know it, perhaps—the sexual objectification of women and so on—came from Europe. But there's too much historical evidence of misogyny as a modus ope-randi in precolonial Africa to associate it only with colonization. In fact, the spiritual power women had in precolonial Africa was often a counterreaction to patriarchal oppression. Although some women had access to power, the "subject" in African society too was male.

Also, I am opposed to all forms of superstitious thinking as methods of knowing because they are grounded in fear. The fa-talistic idea that signs and symbols can determine the outcome of your life detracts from taking responsibility for one's own knowl-edge and capacity to shape life experiences.

Europatriarchal Knowledge may be the biggest obstacle to the well-being of the planet and its inhabitants, but it is not the only one. Neither, to be sure, is Europatriarchal Knowledge synony-mous with white men. You could say that Romantic philosophers, poets, and artists such as Ralph Waldo Emerson, D. H. Lawrence, and Caspar David Friedrich promoted something similar to what I refer to as Sensuous Knowledge in terms of the poetic and the emotional angles they used (certainly not the Afrocentric black feminist one). Take, for example, *Chalk Cliffs on Rügen*, painted by Friedrich as an emotional response to the natural world. In the painting, we see Friedrich and his new bride enjoying a beautiful view of the chalk cliffs in what is now Jasmund National Park in Germany. The work evokes in its viewer a blissful appreciation of nature's beauty.

In the 1920s, the cliffs were threatened by erosion, but protests to ensure their preservation were successful, and the view remains as magical today as it was then. Imagine a world where the chalk cliffs no longer existed. We not only would have lost the chance to see an artful view, we would also miss the opportunity to see the art in ourselves because we are a part of nature. This is what Friedrich himself alluded to when he said, "The artist should paint not only what he sees before him, but also what he sees within him. If, however, he sees nothing within him, then he should also refrain from painting that which he sees before him."

The point is that just as Greek mythology and philosophy have been used for centuries to apply insights to contemporary European life, be it within art, politics, literature, philosophy, or gender relations, the depth to be gained from African myth and philosophy is relevant to all global knowledge.

≡⑴≡⑴≡⑴

We rarely forget ideas that stimulate our senses—historical moments such as Martin Luther King's "I Have a Dream" speech or Nelson Mandela raising his fist when walking out of Robben Island or Ecuador recognizing the rights of nature in its constitution or the composer Ludovico Einaudi performing his hauntingly touching piece of music "Elegy for the Arctic" on a melting glacier in Norway. These moments are exemplary because they affect us wholly—intellectually, emotionally, physically, and spiritually.

The same is true of all good ideas. What an idea makes us feel is just as important as what it makes us know. Good ideas are like good songs, you could say. With the right elements—if the words have cadence, if the voice has beauty and passion, if the "rhythm" of the idea resonates with the zeitgeist—they catch fire and ripple into mainstream culture. As the author and photographer Teju Cole says in an interview with journalist Ryan Kohls on his renowned platform "What I Wanna Know," "There is something deep inside of us that responds to cared for language, whether it's literary, poetry, or really good lyrics in a song."

That said, I end this chapter by emphasizing that Sensuous Knowledge is not some quasi-mystical sixth-sense method of knowing. It is not someone phoning you the moment you think of them. It is not about escaping or aggrandizing the self through magic and mysticism. The theory I am presenting may sound poetic, but a political and urgent concern informs it. It is precisely because we have reason to thank for so much insight that we need to broaden the understanding of knowledge. Because the more we define knowledge with rigid and boxed terms, the more robotic and therefore incapable of actually receiving knowledge people will become.

Nor is the idea that knowledge is an active, embodied process one that I am pulling out from the sky. Even a growing body of scientific work supports the hypothesis. As reported in a *New York Times* article titled "Tales of African American History Found in DNA," studies of African American genetic history show that memory can be passed genetically. The DNA of present-day African Americans reflects the history of living in an apartheid society for generations. As *The Conversation* reports in an article titled "Racism Impacts Your Health" racism affects black people not only psychosocially but also physically. Researchers have found that black people who frequently experience discrimination have higher systolic blood pressure than those who perceive they have been discriminated against very little. Another study found that black women who perceived that they had high rate experiences of racism had increased incidents of breast cancer, and this was especially true among young black women. Biologists are discovering that genomes have more agency than previously thought. We are not only politically and socially disenfranchised by Europatriarchal Knowledge, we are physically scarred by it.

The more we understand knowledge as an ecosystem that reflects interbeing, and that flourishes when our relationships flourish, whether they are relationships with facts, with nature, or with people, the more our world expands. The more we connect with the sensuous, the better we can identify needed political, economic, cultural, and social change.

We have never before believed that knowledge could bring out the best of us. We have never been very good to each other—nor to ourselves or our environment. Understanding this truth is where real change starts. We may have made tremendous advances economically, scientifically, and technologically, but without matching psychological and social progress, those advances have only led us to where we are today—heading toward an environmental, political, and social disaster of dimensions heretofore unimaginable.

A different approach to knowledge would set us on a new path, one that enlightens us both inwardly and outwardly. One in which the insight is informed not only by contained hierarchies, indices, and measurement but also by the nonlinear and interior qualities of the immeasurable. It may sound unrealistic that we'll foster a universal approach to knowledge, but nothing realistic sounding has ever changed the old structures! As the revolutionary and activist Angela Davis says, "You have to act as if it were possible to radically transform the world. And you have to do it all the time."

Ultimately, we cannot become equals unless we are subjects. And we cannot become subjects using Eurocentric, masculinist approaches to epistemology.

of LIBERATION

Laugh and push me down.
Only in song and laughter
I rise again—a black clown.
Strike up the music.
Let it be gay.
Only in joy
Can a clown have his day.

I was stopped in my tracks when I recently read Langston Hughes's poem "*The Black Clown*." The words felt familiar to me, as though they were describing something or someone significant. The poem continued:

God! Give me the spotted
Garments of a clown
So that the pain and the shame
Will not pull me down.
Freedom!

Then it hit me—Lauryn Hill! It was of Ms. Hill that the poem reminded me. The realization made me angsty. Ms. Hill is not a clown, a voice inside my head cautioned. The term *clown* is an insult. It conjures children's party hobo clowns or any slapstick, whimsical character. Not Lauryn, whom I admire.

But once it struck me that from about the mid-2000s, Ms. Hill—whose *Unplugged* album was a life-changing work of art for me—had adopted the clown character for her performances, the matter would not subside. I became fascinated with understanding why the clown archetype was one that seemed to inspire her.

As a mode of critical commentary, the point of clowning is not strictly to entertain and amuse people; it is rather to urge them to open their eyes to deception. The clown wants the world to be better. They may use humor, but ultimately the clown is mocking the bigger structure of trickery rather than the trick. Even the party clown has a subversive side, misleading you while winking at you to let you in on the gag. As the celebrated clown Angela de Castro says, clowns are "truth tellers, entertainers, subversives and communicators in the arts, in society and across the world." Charlie Chaplin, whose anticapitalist political views eventually caused the United States to revoke his reentry permit, also said, "I remain just one thing, and one thing only, and that is a clown. It places me on a far higher plane than any politician."

In her public appearances, Lauryn Hill wears bright, mismatching colors: stripes and checks, oversized baggy coats, and the clown's favorite accessory, a bowler hat. A spectrum of dramatically clashing colors outlines her facial features—greens, yellows, and purples on her eyes, fuchsia cheeks, and red lipstick. At a show in Glasgow in 2018, she wore a buttoned-up red checked dress with large plastic pockets and an oversized black coat draped with see-through latex. A gigantic blue-tinted woolen hat sat loosely on her head, and a bright silver eye shadow that matched her stockings adorned her alert eyes. If ever an artist used fashion to counter rigid notions of womanhood, it is Ms. Hill.

Her look rejects the sexualization of female artists, but it doesn't try to be masculine instead or to do away with sensuality altogether. Ms. Hill still dresses like a woman; she still has feminine sex appeal, but it is not commercially sexualized.

Her movements too are reminiscent of a clown's. She gestures with swift, synthesized, and syncopated motions. Her hands communicate to her band members—rousing them to perform with perfection. She seems less concerned with the audience than with the orchestration of the performance: every cello, every guitar and saxophone is under her control. From clothing to sound, beats to makeup, the details convey as much of a message as her songs themselves do. As she wrote in a blog post on *Medium* a couple of months before the Glasgow show, "I am the architect of my creative expression. No decisions are made without me."

All clowns may know that life is inherently cruel, as Hughes's poem acknowledges, but the black clown also knows that on one side of the tightrope walk is "a white world where cold winds blow." On the other side of the tightrope walk is an audience that does not appreciate the sacrifices the black clown makes to walk to the other end. Instead, the public finds him pitiful, strange, even mad. But if the black clown must feign madness to reject society's warped ideas of sanity, it is a price he finds worth paying. To quote the Japanese film director Akira Kurosawa, "In a mad world, only the mad are sane."

Similarly, the female clown does not primarily aim to be funny. As scholar and clown Anne-Pauline van der A writes in a brilliant essay, "Becoming Annot: Identity Through Clown," where she accounts the evolution of her own clown persona, "The clown has become the means through which the more tragic, modern impulse of the world can be expressed as an insight, a question, or a commentary that is rather more confrontational than it is entertaining. . . ."

In the role of the black *and* female clown, Ms. Hill's performance persona juggles the "cold white world" of the black clown with the "confrontational attitude" of the female clown. In so doing, she aims to open her audience's eyes to the way that a racist, sexist, and capitalist system manipulates them. "Compromise consumerism!" "Rebel!" "Submit to the truth!" she urges, but the audience is there for entertainment, not enlightenment.

Consequently, they feel let down by Ms. Hill. Review after review of the 2018 tour complained that the songs from *The Miseducation of Lauryn Hill,* the album that she performed that year, were unrecognizable. Following critical comments from audiences, Ms. Hill once tried to explain that her behavior comes from a place of good intention. "To those supporters who were told that I abandoned them, that is untrue," she said. "I abandoned greed, corruption, and compromise, never you, and never the artistic gifts and abilities that sustained me." Perhaps, if the novelist and essayist James Baldwin were a witness to these exchanges, he would remind us of his words in the essay "The Creative Process": "Societies never know it, but the war of an artist with his society is a lover's war, and he does, at his best, what lovers do, which is to reveal the beloved to himself and, with that revelation, to make freedom real."

Still, since the release of her 2001 *Unplugged 2.0* album, in particular, accusations of lunacy have stalked the character of Ms. Hill like a shadow. The *Los Angeles Times* reviewed the album as "unhinged," and a *Guardian* write-up about it was titled "Songs from La-La Land." Even her former partner and band member, Wyclef Jean, told the *Rolling Stone* that "she needs psychiatric help."

To me, *Unplugged* was the most beautiful thing I'd ever heard. Like everyone, I waxed enthusiastic about Ms. Hill's previous album, *The Miseducation of Lauryn Hill*. However, unlike most people around me, when *Unplugged* was released, I took to it even more. The album was not only a melodious treat, it was enlightening. Ms. Hill raised issues that few mainstream artists dared to, such as systemic racial oppression and the music industry's manipulative ways. She spoke about reclaiming her love for music from an industry that took it away. Most significantly, she talked about liberation. In its entirety, *Unplugged* is one of the strongest treatises for liberation ever created. Every single song on the album speaks to perceiving the deceptions and delusions that prevent freedom of the mind and soul, which is what liberation ultimately is.

Not only did she speak about liberation, she also evoked it. The album's depth lay not merely in her words, profound as they were, but also in their genuineness. As Ms. Hill encouraged people to unlearn everything they know and to reject a "decaying social system," she was herself clearly in the process of unlearning everything *she* knew and saying goodbye to a decaying system.

It is hardly unusual that the cultural establishment ridicules female artists who are critical of systemic injustices, including those within the music industry. Artists like Alanis Morissette, Joss Stone, Sinéad O'Connor, Fiona Apple, and Pussy Riot have also received varying degrees of flak for being allegedly "delusional," "misjudging," and "man-hating." Black female artists such as Ms. Hill, or Billie Holiday and Nina Simone, or Nigerian artist Nneka and South African singer Simphiwe Dana after her—women who speak truth to power—face double the ridicule and demonization. They are associated not only with "female" irrationality and hysteria but also with having a racial chip on their shoulder. Even when Lauryn Hill spoke out against something as reprehensible as pedophilia during a visit to the Vatican, the press turned an act of bravery into yet another accusation of her instability. Had she been a white male artist, she just might have won a peace prize for such a bold statement. As the South African feminist scholar Pumla Dineo Gqola writes in a book about Simphiwe Dana (*A Renegade Called Simphiwe*), "You need to know what you are doing, especially if you are a woman, and be quite assertive because in this industry people first tune into you because of your difference but they soon try to turn you into what they think makes sense."

Ms. Hill's affirmations that she would get out of the boxes imposed on her became critical knowledge, which I listened to tirelessly, day in, day out. She didn't package her philosophy into a neat studio album ready for consumption. For it to ring true, it had to be delivered intimate and raw. In Hill's hands, I felt like I was a lump of dough, first being fermented, then expanded, then rising. The process was erotic, in the sense that Audre Lorde defines the erotic—as "in the way my body stretches to music and opens in response." Ms. Hill's mellifluous guitar combined with her honeyed voice seduced me into a state where I imbibed the juice of knowledge that poured into my mind. It was Sensuous Knowledge at its purest.

Questions about liberation were at the forefront of my mind when *Unplugged* was released. As a child, all I ever wanted to be when I grew up was a liberated woman. Something in me knew that if I became a free and fearless woman, then everything else would be all right. However, my sociocultural education had insisted on teaching me to fear the woman I wanted to become, and I'd complied. But that same year, 2001, I had an experience with automatic writing—when you write unstoppably and feverishly as though controlled by an external force—which inadvertently set me on a path to pursuing my childhood dream.

There might be other ways than channeling external energy to describe the spell of automatic writing that occurred that night and on occasions to follow. But at the time, the event troubled—no, terrified—me enough to seek out information. My search to understand the experience led me to people like Dag Hammarskjöld, Neale Donald Walsch, John Yeats, and Simone Weil, who also experienced automatic writing. I read them to understand the mystical phenomenon, but in between the contemplative lines of their words, I instead found a practice of meditation.

Once I began meditating, I slowly began to question all the social norms I held. First, I called into question the validity of the religion I'd chosen to believe in as a child. I say "chosen," for when I was nine years old, I decided to become a Catholic. My mother, a recovering Protestant from Finland, and my father, a secular Yoruba Muslim, were not in a position to help with my newfound Roman-inspired religion. However, being an interfaith family, they humored me when I decided to go to Sunday worship with family and friends, rightly knowing that I would soon be bored and think of more fun ways to spend my day off. But I continued to believe in the white, male Christian God into my twenties, when I (automatically, you could say) wrote my way out of that belief.

Once I questioned religion, I began to question every other authority in my life. It was like a Russian matryoshka doll. I'd strip bare one layer of conditioning, only to discover another, nearly identical, one inside it. Once I expelled the God Authority, there was the White Authority, then the Male Authority, later the Society Authority, then the Family Authority. With each authority decreasing in size and importance, the matryoshka doll grew tinier and tinier. The smaller all the authorities became, the more I felt connected to the quality that had tugged at me since childhood—freedom.

But liberation was like the sun gleaming through a tree but still obscured by the tree's trunk, branches, and leaves. I had forests of dogma to wade through. I grew up in Nigeria, the world's largest black nation consisting of cultures where women once had near-divine, if still confined, status. Yet my upbringing taught me that God was white and male. In school I learned that a Scottish explorer named Mungo Park discovered the Niger, my country's primary river. Long before Park was born and before the Europa-triarchal invasion of West Africa, this river, which sustained West African kingdoms, was referred to by locals as N'geren'geo in some parts of West Africa, Joliba and Quorra in others. I learned that girls should be nice even when boys misbehaved because they were "being boys." I was taught to covet material things that my wealthy friends had access to, although frankly I was never too bothered with that in particular. I learned that it was nature's order that men had all the so-called head positions in society. They were "heads" of state, "heads" of companies, "heads" of the army, and "heads" of families.

When a military regime caused my mother and me to tempo-rarily relocate to Sweden when I was a teenager, the brainwashing continued. In my new school I was taught, with varying degrees of subtlety, that Africans were uncivilized and primitive. I learned that my skin color was enough to make people attack me verbally and physically. I learned that my brown skin and bushy hair were considered unattractive.

Later, when I moved to New York, then London, I learned that the consequence of bringing up topics such as racism and sex-ism was the accusation of being militant.

Everywhere I lived, the message was the same. Women should not express their sexuality, not voice their opinions, not show anger. Men are innately more rational, more sexual, more assertive, more autonomous. In the time I had lived on this planet, I was taught by patriarchy and white supremacy to subdue, hate, compare, judge, undervalue, condemn, and ultimately destroy myself.

And for a long time, I complied. Despite being raised in what you could call a modern *agbe-ile* (family compound) with traditional customs around me, nurtured by socialist and Pan-African parents who cited Malcolm X and Bertolt Brecht, sang agitprop, and fed me ideas about liberation, I was loyal to my sociocultural education.

I uncritically absorbed accounts of how Europe discovered everything from the River Niger to the Egyptian pyramids to Africa itself during its fifteenth-century expansive voyages. I didn't know that African kingdoms sent delegates to fifteenth-century Europe too. Great empires such as Benin, Ashanti, Kongo, and Ethiopia established embassies in Europe to amass power back home. I knew that European elites expropriated African art to raise their status but not that they commissioned artworks such as the Afro-Portuguese ivories made in Guinea-Bissau, Sierra Leone, Congo, and Nigeria. Europeans, who never invented an alphabet (the modern alphabet being of Semitic origin), still diminished Africans by arguing they lacked writing, even though Africans were the first people to invent writing in ancient Egypt, and they invented at least four alphabets with distinct characters and phonetic symbols, such as the Vai syllabary in Sierra Leone or the Igbo Nsibidi alphabet. Similarly, although we are educated that the best writers are male, the first known writer in history was Enheduanna, a Sumerian high priestess. When Africa, blackness, or womanhood were attacked, however subtly, I didn't always defend them for fear that I would alienate a colleague, friend, or family member. (And on the occasions I did that was just what happened, and it was exhausting.) But the more I resisted, the more I realized that to change society, one must first change oneself. But to change myself, I did not merely need new knowledge; I needed a new understanding of knowledge.

Like Ms. Hill I determined to become like "one of those mad scientists" who tests theories on themselves first to affirm that they work before sharing them with others. Like Ms. Hill I also learned such an endeavor would be a challenge. It would mean "learning by way of experience" and not giving up when "you're making mistakes."

My character as a child already was feminist, if in an inward, old-womanly sense rather than an outward, tomboyish one. But still, I accepted lousy behavior from boys, and later men, because they were "being boys." I recall one lover whose hot-cold treatment I tolerated because, after all, when he was in his hot mode, we were *so* compatible. And another whom I dotingly loved despite that he habitually sulked whenever something extraordinary happened to me. Any cause to celebrate on my part was a cause to whine on his. What a waste of youthful zest!

When I stopped putting up with such outright lousy behavior, I still did most of the emotional work in my relationships—that is, until I realized that men depend on women for emotional needs, which they lack the honesty to admit that they have. The problem patriarchal society has with women is not when we oppose patriarchy intellectually but rather precisely when we act according to our opposition emotionally. It is much more acceptable for a woman to speak out against patriarchal norms, such as women being the ones who create space for intimacy in a relationship, than for her to actively stop taking responsibility for that work. This is not to suggest that making behavioural changes rooted in feminine autonomy is easy. It's always a process marked by a kind of experimentation because it has no representation in culture; there are few depictions of genuinely reciprocal relationships, for example.

But there are realizations from which you can never return, light-bulb moments that shape your destiny by revealing the constellations of your behavior. When I ceased taking responsibility for the emotional side of a love affair, especially in the early stages of a relationship, either the relationship would evaporate into thin air or the boyfriend would sulk or throw a tantrum (yes, men have emotions). That women's emotional expression is so central to upholding male dominance in the heterosexual institution (social norms that inform heterosexual relationships) was the one truth above any other that undid the already shaky structure the institution held in my mind. Once it collapsed, it left behind a void. At first I felt disoriented—who was I if I didn't seek the safety and stability of relationship? How did the romantic in me feel about my disinterest in the romantic ideals that thus far provided her with psychological well-being?—but over time, that void was replaced with a space where, instead of viewing relationship as a fixed destination, there was a corresponding opportunity for relationship to be a cherished but not essential part of life. Relationship was only valuable to me if it encouraged both the lover and me to become our "higher selves," a message Ms. Hill beautifully conveys in "I Gotta Find Peace of Mind."

By the time I settled into adulthood, I'd normalized the discord between my ideal self and the self that society pushed me into becoming. Not that I was a docile Goody Two-shoes. I spoke back at racists (if more quickly than at sexists). I read my Walter Rodney and Noam Chomsky and listened to my Tracy Chapman and Talib Kweli. I got a bachelor's degree in political science and read feminist books. I experimented with drugs. I broke hearts obliviously (until someone returned the favor). I explored my sexuality uninhibitedly, traveled and lived in exciting cities around the world, I moved to Spain to learn a new language, and built a career in the creative industries.

My life was adventurous and exciting. But even the excitement belonged to the script of my cultural education. After all, modern culture expects, if not recommends, that young people wild out before settling into conformity. Deep in my heart, I knew that the little feminist girl who once dreamed of liberation was far from achieving her dream.

I wished nothing but to write, travel, study, teach, fall in love on my terms, again and again, if with the same person, have no children (including no man-child), and advocate for liberation. I wanted to live my theory, to make choices based on my philosophy—liberation. But how could I when I still had so far to go in freeing myself? For a long time I could not even bring myself to vocalize these desires. Whenever I tried, I was met with misunderstanding and discomfort at best. At worst, I lost friends, family, and lovers. To avoid the constant battle between my truth and my socialization, I sensed myself slipping into the adult life that I'd once dreaded—a life shaped by others' expectations. I was too insecure and terrified to do anything about it.

When we live in ways that please others but not ourselves "a part of us dies" Ms. Hill said in her contemplative "Interlude 1." By 2009 my physical health had taken a toll from the stress of working in a Europatriarchal environment, and my mental health seemed to be next in line. I'd often come home from work late at night and collapse in tears on the couch from sheer exhaustion. As Ms. Hill might say, I'd submitted to someone else's (society's) opinion, and a part of me had died.

One morning I went to work anticipating a regular, dreadful day, but before the workday ended, I'd spontaneously resigned. Not long after, I left a long-term relationship, also unforeseen. My friends were surprised and concerned—legitimately, I might add. It was at the height of the recession. I had just bought property. I barely had any savings, and I couldn't rely on my parents to pay my mortgage. But none of it bothered me. I wrote all day every day, and I felt freer than ever.

My spontaneity was, however, made possible by two key things: class privilege and the meditation practice I'd cultivated throughout my twenties. Class privilege meant that although neither my childhood nor early adulthood was spent in affluence, I didn't feel deprived at this time of anything but luxury and splendor, which were not things I craved anyway. Also, my dual heritage afforded me a sense of worldliness. Most people in the world cannot make whim decisions based on inner dissatisfaction. The majority of humanity *must* do work that they hate doing whether they like it or not.

The more I meditated—meditation being the only time when we are not distracted by something or someone else—the better I got to know myself. The better I got to know myself, the less I felt I had to lose in being authentic. The less I felt I had to lose, the freer I became. In "Me and Bobby McGee," Janis Joplin sang about how freedom was synonymous with "nothing left to lose." It may sound bleak but the "nothing," as I interpret it, means things like status, appearance, and approval.

In March 2010 I launched my blog, *MsAfropolitan*, and subsequently a career as a pan-African feminist commentator. I wrote what I longed to read: attention-grabbing articles about topics that weren't being discussed sufficiently if at all.

At the core were questions such as: What does it mean to be oppressed? What does it mean to be liberated? Why do women choose to follow authority even when they have the option to be autonomous? What is the cost of compromising one's true self? Is there a true self? What narratives particularly subjugate women and people of African heritage? And what kinds of stories can heal and empower?

Liberation is like the southern African story about the lion that grew up in a flock of sheep and didn't know that she was a lion. She bleated like a sheep and ate grass like a sheep. One day the herd was wandering in the jungle when a mighty lion leaped out of the forest. As the sheep scattered away from her, the jungle lion saw the other lion there among the sheep. She chased it down. "What are you doing here?" she asked. And the sheep-lion said, "Have mercy on me. Don't eat me. Please." The jungle lion dragged her to a lake and told her to look at the water. The lion who thought she was a sheep looked at the water and saw her reflection, then looked at the jungle lion, then looked at her reflection again, and then let out a mighty roar. She would never be a sheep again. She was what Ms. Hill titled "The Conquering Lion."

The system built upon Europatriarchal Knowledge seldom regards music as having the potential to speak to questions of deeper historiographical and philosophical significance. As Plato said, "It is very dangerous to allow the wrong kind of music in the republic."

Nigerian composer Fela Kuti said, by contrast, "I consider music to be effective like a weapon to inform people." For black people in modern history, music is one of the first sources through which we learn to think critically. It is through music that we first learn that the educational system does not provide the knowledge of resistance that we need to survive. When we listen to artists such as Bob Marley, Tracy Chapman, Wu-Tang Clan, Marvin Gaye, Fela Kuti, Nipsey Hussle, Salt-N-Pepa, and Miriam Makeba, we are not simply bopping along; we are in school taking notes. Music also connects us intergenerationally and cross-geographically. What we hear in hip-hop, older generations heard in the soul of Motown, in the jazz of the Harlem Renaissance, in the calypso and the Nyabinghi.

Unplugged belongs to the same tradition of Audre Lorde's *Sister Outsider*, Alice Walker's *In Search of Our Mothers' Gardens*, and bell hooks's *Wounds of Passion, Sisters of the Yam*, and *All About Love,* books that I have read over and over again but in which I always discover something new. Books with that multilayered quality of truth telling, poetry, and nourishing that constitutes "blackwomanness." The Cuban-Jamaican poet from Brooklyn, Aja Monet, whose work also exists in this category of art, describes black womanhood as a kind of magic that isn't easily "hashtagged" in her poem "#SayHerName." But insofar as hashtags represent a mode of creative archiving, perhaps we could draw inspiration from Ghanaian poet Abena Busia's poem "Liberation" for a meaning to blackwomanness. Busia conjures an image of powerful and fiery women whose "tears of knowledge" can nevertheless beautify life with laughter.

To inspire originally meant "to draw in spirit." Music makes the process of critical learning like a long and refreshing inhale that you "draw through spirit." In Swedish, the word for spirituality, *andlig,* reflects this view perfectly. A literal translation of *andlig* means "breath-like."

Osho, the Indian spiritual guru, said, "If a Buddha is not misunderstood then he is not a Buddha at all." A comparison between Ms. Hill and the notion of the Buddha may seem disproportionate. But I am speaking of *a buddha,* which simply means an enlightened one, rather than *the Buddha.* There are also similarities between a buddha and inspiring figures such as the Indian philosopher Jiddu Krishnamurti, who rejected his appointment as a messiah for the more thankless but meaningful work of challenging people to think differently. Or the Afrobeat legend Fela Kuti, who, like Ms. Hill, rejected the commercializing and commodifying music industry. In an interview following an eighteen-month prison sentence, Kuti said, "I'm very spiritually inclined, and prison gave me a lot of time to meditate and think about what this world is really about." He predictively explained that he rejected the industry because "African music was going to be the music of the future, even in Europe, so I didn't want to participate in the madness of commercialism, I didn't want to participate in the madness of gimmicks, I didn't want African music to belong to the fashion where music comes and goes." As Osho continued, "The Buddha has to say the unsayable, he has to express the inexpressible, he has to define the indefinable."

The Ghanaian poet Kofi Awoonor aptly said, "Freedom is a very difficult word to pin down." However, there is one thing we can say about it: freedom is not the absence of suffering, it is the absence of suffering from being yourself. Suffering is part of the human experience, but to suffer from being yourself is a condition, that as I have tried to convey in this chapter with Ms. Hill's *Unplugged* album as a companion, is caused to a great extent by the varying ways in which the social system indoctrinates you. Freedom is the ability to perceive and subsequently destabilize the indoctrination. Freedom is to not forget who you are and what you stand for as Ms. Hill too urges in "So Much Things to Say." However, freedom is also undertaking this journey lightly.

In African knowledge systems, a mask often represents an ideal. Masks used by the women's Sande society, for example, represent ideals of female beauty for the Mende. As the African worldview rarely distinguishes between aesthetic and inner beauty, masks also represent spiritual paragons.

African masks, like all art, are driven by emotion, but here the art is not the African mask itself but rather the masked performance. Displaying an African mask at a museum is akin to exhibiting Leonardo da Vinci's paintbrush at the Louvre. The product itself is missing. It is when a dancer impersonates the message of the mask that the art is produced.

I mention this because although the mask is typically perceived as a symbol of concealment and insecurity, I urge you to think of a mask differently—as an opportunity for reinvention, awakening, and the shedding of the old. The mask reflects one of the important truths about freedom—there is no fixed, authentic self. Who you are today is not who you must be tomorrow. The worship of consistency is a prison and when you step out of the prison, you can leave the oppressive narrative it imposed on you behind. As Frantz Fanon said, "In the world through which I travel, I am endlessly creating myself."

When a clown is in character, they are similarly creating a self that is inseparable from their performance. In the embodiment of clown, they transcend social expectations and social norms. They break codes and conventions. They deceive to teach. They teach that a lack of self-knowledge and social awareness is dangerous. By giving human form to the clown archetype, the clown becomes a kind of buddha that expresses the inexpressible, as Osho said.

In his wonderful book, "The Face", the author Chris Abani refers to how the face in Afikpo culture, where his roots lie, "is a stage, a state of flux, of becoming." In this manner, the face is seen as a performance which gives life to the consciousness of the wearer. Abani continues to say, "It is important to wear the right face."

This is how we should think of liberation too. Liberation is a reinvention of the self. It is wearing the right face; masks that peel away layers of dogma to reveal the kernel of who we are and desire to be. It is possible as Ms. Hill repeats again and again in *Unplugged*, and yet as Hughes's clown archetypically returns to say, we will fall again and again too, "But no! Not forever like this will I be, here are my hands that can really make me free!"

of DECOLONIZATION

Sometimes writing turns into fear. I fear writing, for I hardly know if the words I am using are my salvation or my dishonor. It seems that everything around me was, and still is, colonialism.

—Grada Kilomba

It is about time we started singing about our own heroic deeds.

—Buchi Emecheta

If you pick up one end of the stick, you also pick up the other.

—Ethiopian proverb

Some years ago I met a Ghanaian man whom we can call Anthony. Little about this affair was unusual as far as heritage is concerned. Inadvertently, all but one of my steady relationships have been with West Africans—Nigerians and Ghanaians, to be precise. But Anthony was the first West African I had a relationship with who had a common British name.

Given the topic of the chapter, decolonization, it may seem that I thought his British name implied a colonized mind. But our encounter led me to discover that *I* was the one still grappling with the effects of colonization. Because despite asking him to tell me his Ghanaian name—Akwesi—so that I could call him that, I stuck to Anthony.

It just seemed forced to suddenly swap the name he had introduced himself with for a name I had requested on semipolitical grounds. I felt as though I'd asked him to put on an Afro wig and a kente robe and act natural.

When the reverse happens to me, and people ask my Yoruba name, then proceed always to call me Abiola, or my Muslim name, Rashidat, I somewhat appreciate the gesture of honoring a shared legacy, but I also feel awkward to be called anything than the name I go by, Minna.

The situation brought up a dilemma. Neither name rolled easily off my tongue anymore. I was just as self-conscious when I called him Anthony as I was when I called him Akwesi. Worse, I didn't settle on Anthony or Akwesi. I seesawed from name to name as though choosing between chocolates in a box, making it all the more amusing.

The experience nevertheless alludes to colonial legacies. How long does a name remain colonial? Could one not argue that *Anthony* is by now as much of a Ghanaian name as *Antonio* is a Mexican name or *Anton* a Scandinavian one? Or is it the case that Africa, as the continent of black heritage, should stick to indigenous names? And was my discomfort in switching names about merely getting to know someone as *A* and then struggling to think of them suddenly as *B*, or was it connected to a more deep-rooted crisis of identity?

One thing the experience shone a light on is that colonial legacy interferes not only with geopolitical relationships but also with interpersonal relationships. It interferes, in other words, with matters of the mind, body, and soul. The most seemingly mundane things, such as what to call a lover, are complicated because of the history of colonization.

Questions about naming and language have indeed shaped much of the debate about decolonization to date. In the groundbreaking book *Decolonising the Mind* by Kenyan novelist and intellectual Ngũgĩ wa Thiong'o, which continues to shape much of the decolonization debate, he argued that the suppression of African languages is the root cause of mental colonization. As Thiong'o piercingly wrote, "The bullet was the means of the physical subjugation. Language was the means of the spiritual subjugation."

Thiong'o declared that he would no longer write in English, and he provokingly argued that what is considered African literature is actually Afro-European literature. (Ouch.) Such bold insights contribute to why *Decolonising the Mind* is one of the strongest books of resistance ever written. It sharply conveys what it means to exist as a colonized person in the world, which is how the vast majority of the world's populace exists.

But what sets the book apart is that it gives voice to the African peasantry. Thiong'o's conveyance of class resistance in the book is one of the most powerful and beautiful ever written in the socialist struggle. In a chapter titled "The Language of African Theatre," Thiong'o portrays the making of a play titled *Ngaahika Ndeenda* ("I Will Marry When I Want"). The story centers on a peasant farmer, Kĩgũũnda; his wife, Wangechi; and their daughter, Gathoni. The family is expecting a surprise visit from a wealthy businessman, Ahab Kĩoi wa Kanoru, for whom Kĩgũũnda works. As they speculate whether the purpose of the visit may be that Kanoru's son is keen to ask Gathoni's hand in marriage, the pair reminisce about the days of their own courtship.

"The music of our language gave us a view of the world, but it has a beauty of its own," Thiong'o wrote. Although Thiong'o was still writing in English at the time, the play, which he coauthored with Kenyan-Zimbabwean playwright Ngugi wa Mirii, certainly brings out a melody that seems innate to Gikuyu. Poetic metaphors in the chapter, such as "teeth which seemed to be washed with milk," "breasts pointed like the tip of the sharpest thorn," and "a body slim and straight like the eucalyptus" leave the reader with the petrichor of village life. There is a splendor in these lines, a look inward that transports me to Kamiriithu, where the play took place.

The language of the people is as urgent to bring to the fore today as it was when Thiong'o wrote the book in 1986. It is perhaps more pressing even, considering that despite all Africa's resources, Africa, according to statistical indexes, is still the poorest continent in terms of people's access to basic amenities. The West's military interventions, resource exploitation, NGO propaganda, unjustifiable debt and trade policies, and other neocolonial practices still have devastating effects on African states' abilities to cope with health and infrastructure development. But poverty is also very much about decolonizing the mind. Neocolonialism has impeded the development of consciousness through adequate educational systems. As a result, African societies have been unable to naturally progress so that their systems of law, agriculture, intracontinental trade, indigenous health care, and philosophical outlook have kept pace with the needs of citizens. Using examples such as *Ngaahika Ndeenda*, Thiong'o convincingly argued that decolonization must raise the question of poverty to the fore.

Yet it is also in "The Language of African Theatre" chapter that *Decolonising the Mind*, like much of the decolonization discussions, fails to fully advocate the end of deception and delusion, which is what mental decolonization is all about. One gets the sense that decolonization of the mind will come at the cost of women. Traditional patriarchal institutions, for example, are represented as intrinsic to decolonized Kenyan nationhood. Wangechi is the "little maiden" who will cultivate the land belonging to Kīgūūnda. If you read the full play, you discover that when things go wrong for Gathoni, following her choice to dress in Western clothes—referred to by the characters as the "fineries of a whore"—and to marry the son of the wealthy businessman in a Christian wedding, the criticism of modernity and Westernization is placed upon the body of a young woman. The reader begins to blame Gathoni for the demise of traditional values. Instead of questioning the hunger for power in both traditional and modern patriarchies, the story typically assigns it to women to biologically, culturally, and symbolically protect patriarchal traditions.

Time is a relentless judge, but art is a conversation with its times and should therefore be evaluated in the context in which it was produced. Thiong'o wrote the book at a time when the feminist struggle had not yet shaped black and African narratives as influentially as it does today. However, the historic World Conference on Women took place in Kenya in 1985, when Thiong'o would have been writing the book. So it is justifiable to wonder why the book shows little evidence of feminist interventions.

Nor is it my intention to enshrine Thiong'o's book as the pinnacle of all literary efforts to end mental colonization. As seminal as it is to modern discussions of the theme and to my own thinking, the type of action that the phrase "decolonization of the mind" connotes goes back at the very least to people such as W. E. B. Du Bois, Marcus Garvey, and African World War I and II veterans such as Barack Obama's grandfather, Hussein Onyango Obama, who returned to the continent with an anticolonial sentiment.

Before it was called decolonization, there were already efforts to alter the mind-set of the masses from a submissive to a defiant stance. There was the Haitian Revolution, which was the revolt led by Toussaint L'Ouverture in Saint-Domingue, which resulted in the creation of an independent Haiti in 1791. There was the 1835 Malê Revolt against enslavement in Brazil (inspired by the Haitian Revolution), and the Matale Rebellion in Sri Lanka led by peasants. These are just a fraction of liberation struggles that contained an element of mental decolonization, which is to say that they strove not only to recover geographical but also psychological territory. Movements such as Pan-Africanism, Hindu nationalism, the Civil Rights Movement—all arguably decolonization movements—were in many ways continuations of the above struggles.

Also, while *Decolonising the Mind* spoke to the black African context in particular, the problem it addressed was relevant in every land that had been colonized, which of course was almost everywhere. This was clear from the literature written both before and after Thiong'o's classic—compelling books such as the incisive thinker Frantz Fanon's *Wretched of the Earth* (1961), political theorist Edward Said's *Orientalism* (1978), and philosopher Walter Mignolo's *The Idea of Latin America* (2005), among many others.

There was also the song by the king of Afrobeat, Fela Kuti, titled "*Colonial Mentality*" or "colomentality," as it became known in short. Released in 1977, the song said that colomentality is a mental state found when the colonial occupation of African land has ceased but the colonial rule of the African mind continues. As Kuti put it in Pidgin English, "Dem don release you nau but you neva release yourself."

Although my generation still faced our own share of mental colonization, it is unfathomable to many of us what earlier generations experienced. My father, for example, studied in Yoruba until standard two (second grade), when suddenly he and his peers were physically punished if they spoke Yoruba in school. They were castigated by well-meaning African teachers who themselves had been brainwashed into thinking that English was the superior language that would help them to succeed in life. This despite how Yoruba intellectually enriches English, as is obvious to anyone who carefully observes the English of a dual Yoruba-English speaker. Just read a book by Wole Soyinka, for example, to see what I mean. This is what Thiong'o, who, like my father, studied in his native language, Gikuyu, for his first educative years, means when he writes that "the physical violence of the battlefield was followed by the psychological violence of the classroom." The condemning of indigenous languages played a huge role in Europatriarchal colonization. Therefore, strengthening indigenous languages must play a seminal role in decolonizing the mind.

Yet the language in which we decolonize the mind is less important than the ideas involved in the process. Just because you speak Hausa, Wolof, Kiswahili, or Zulu does not mean you have decolonized your mind. We all know people who speak one or more indigenous languages but who by no means have progressive minds. At the same time, we all know people—ancestors such as Frantz Fanon and Toni Morrison—who spoke only a colonial language and yet serve as inspirations of a decolonized mind.

Of course, there are dead ends in thinking about the decolonization of the mind if you think only in English, French, Spanish, Arabic, or Portuguese. I've reached them myself while researching Yoruba philosophy, for example. Not speaking Yoruba limits my ability to draw out the information that I need to craft theory that I yearn to craft. Naturally, if you are fluent in a native language *and* you cultivate a decolonized state of mind, then you are in an advantageous position. But how you approach decolonizing your thinking is more important than in which language you do it. What matters when it comes to decolonization is that it must not be Europatriarchy in blackface. In the twenty-first century, decolonizing the mind cannot be the same repackaging of patriarchy with Pan-Africanism. For example, Fela's song "Colonial Mentality" spoke exclusively to the colonized man. As the feminist poet Adrienne Rich said, "This is the oppressor's language. Yet I need it to talk to you."

In Nigeria there was an incentive to create a new common language known as GBORUSA, an acronym formed from (I)gbo, (Yo)ru(ba), and (Hau)sa, which are the three main languages in the country. But I am not convinced that it would be a decolonial project in the holistic sense of challenging patriarchy, heteronormativity (the belief that heterosexuality is the normal expression of sexuality), and elitism. I'm reminded of the creation of Esperanto, the universal language, an otherwise profoundly humanist endeavor that cannot help us now because its founder was unaware of his gender and race biases.

Also, although the language many of us speak is technically English or French, etc., I'd argue that we speak several forms of it. Although I speak "English" with my dad and elder family members, it sounds completely different from the "English" I speak elsewhere. I mentally switch to another language in the same way that I do if I speak Finnish, Swedish, Pidgin English, German, or Spanish.

When it comes to the mind, decolonization will succeed only when it is clear once and for all that the colonial mind is a mind that is invaded by a whole network of synergetic efforts to prevent clarity so that it continues to enact servitude. It is like a computer—if you protect it only from malware, it can still be infested with a virus or be vulnerable to phishing. You have to guard your files against the network of exploiters.

The method of monopolizing power is always the same. Take away people's rights, with violence if necessary; deprive them of economic resources; and manipulate culture and tradition to justify your actions.

The colonizer imposes their language, religion, ideologies, and narrative and uses violent tactics such as detention without trial, collective punishment, mass execution, forced resettlement, and extreme torture to occupy geographical and psychological territory. The patriarch uses similar violent tactics to colonize women's bodies and minds. He uses domestic violence, female genital mutilation, foot binding, breast ironing, forced abortion, witch trials, dowries, honor killings, sexual assault, rape, corrective rape, forced prostitution, sexual slavery, widow punishment, sexual objectification, misogynist pornography, and respectability politics.

In 1987 the Pan-Africanist, Marxist, and feminist Burkinabé revolutionary Thomas Sankara delivered a speech to a rally of several thousand women in Ouagadougou, the capital city of Burkina Faso. In "The Revolution Cannot Triumph Without the Emancipation of Women," he said,

Posing the question of women in Burkinabé society today means posing the abolition of the system of slavery to which they have been subjected for millennia. The first step is to try to understand how this system works, to grasp its real nature in all its subtlety, in order then to work out a line of action that can lead to women's total emancipation. In other words, in order to win this battle that men and women have in common, we must be familiar with all aspects of the woman question on a world scale and here in Burkina. We must understand how the struggle of the Burkinabé woman is part of a worldwide struggle of all women and, beyond that, part of the struggle for the full rehabilitation of our continent. Thus, women's emancipation is at the heart of the question of humanity itself, here and everywhere.

Sankara grasped that the decolonization of the masses can succeed only if it simultaneously emphasizes the liberation of women, because "sexism," as Toni Morrison said in "The Source of Self-Regard, is "the oldest class oppression in the world." Sankara's vision remains unique among the critical shapers of decolonization. Not only is it unique, it is brave, for this is a view that has repeatedly been contested.

Throughout African history, women's roles in resistance have been essential yet diminished. The very same year that Nigeria was formed, in 1914, tens of thousands of women staged a protest, which the African feminist scholar Nwando Achebe has referred to as the "Ogidi Palaver," in her book "Shaping Our Struggles: Nigerian Women in History." It was a protest in the market against both indigenous and British men who together had sidelined them in decision making. Yet these stories are not part of the Afropatriarchal (if I may invent yet a term) narrative. It makes you wonder, which struggle are black women and men fighting together? Is it black liberation or black male liberation?

Fortunately, systems of oppression are disintegrating like never before. If ever there were a time when male supremacists cannot ignore women's voices, it is now. All over the world, feminists are exposing the inhumane ways that patriarchy oppresses women—and men too.

Consequently, contemporary forms of the decolonization debate are also taking feminist questions into account. Campaigns such as Rhodes Must Fall started at the University of Cape Town when students took down a statue of the colonizer Cecil Rhodes. It marked the beginning of a worldwide conversation about decolonizing knowledge in higher education and has brought questions about patriarchy and sexism to the fore.

In Bolivia the Vice Ministry of Decolonization aims to help Bolivia recover from its five hundred years under colonial rule. The department includes a Depatriarchalization Unit currently headed by Elisa Vega Sillo, a former leader in the indigenous campesina women's movement and a campaigner against machismo and patriarchy. These are results of feminist campaigns that raise awareness that decolonization and patriarchy cannot prosper simultaneously.

In New Zealand, the Whanganui River was granted the same legal rights as a person, becoming the first river in the world to be recognized as a living entity. It is a significant moment in decolonization when we step away from the anthropocentric bias and begin to conduct a reciprocal dialogue with the natural sources of life. Rivers are very friendly to us. The least we can do is try to have a "conversation" with them and ask what rivers want in order to feel good. To do this we need to recognize them as living entities.

If decolonization movements are to truly succeed, it will depend on language all right, but the big language question today is whether we will approach decolonization in the characteristic robotic and soulless way of Europatriarchal Knowledge or if the language we use will itself reflect the outcome we seek.

We ought to be mindful not to speak of decolonization of the mind using the "master's tools," as though it can be measured and assessed through some formula.

There is no magic pill that you swallow to wake up with a decolonized mind the next day. There is no scientific test you can take to affirm the level of your decolonization.

We also speak of decolonization as though the prefix *de-* means to amputate wrong thoughts from your mind. But you cannot extract colonial thinking by forcefully removing parts of your character and behavior. The mind does not work that way. You cannot just remove thoughts as one might get rid of old furniture. All such attempts result only in self-censorship, collective deception, and paranoia.

Decolonization of the mind should instead cause a sense of unity and calm in the mind. It is not removing thought patterns by force but instead gently inserting new insights, which eventually reshuffle and do away with harmful thoughts.

Imagine the mind as a garden. Our traditional idea of decolonizing it would be like vigorously chopping down a poison ivy that is threatening to infest the garden with its toxic branches. But decolonizing the garden of the mind is more about planting new, rare, forgotten, and hybrid trees, herbs, and flowers that eventually do away with the ivy. It is decorating the trees with bowls where birds can rest and sing songs of freedom. It is creating a wild meadow in the center of the enclave and finding time to just lie in this green place.

While lying in the garden of the mind, it is it, observing how every poisoned bark and every blooming bud find a way to exist in this enclosure together. Meditating in the garden of the mind means noting what is real and what is false. It means tending to the recovery and recuperation of lost memory and self-value. Decolonizing the mind is a process of inserting and reinserting, imagining and reimagining, shaping and reshaping. It is ultimately creating something new using what is needed from the past.

It is like the Japanese *kintsugi*, also known as "golden repair," the art of repairing a broken glass object with powdered gold. In *kintsugi*, the gilded cracks give the piece character and beauty.

Decolonization of the mind is using powdered gold not only to heal the mind but also to turn trauma into strength.

In 2016, as a visiting lecturer and writing fellow at Hong Kong Baptist University, I came across a poster by the entrance to the school's institute of Chinese medicine that made me pause. It said, "Learn from the past but not to be confined to it; learn from the west but not to abandon our own."

They were the words of the nineteenth-century sage and physician Zhang Xichun, considered a master of medicine in China. He was speaking about health care, but his words could refer to decolonization as well. Decolonization is not about a return to precolonial times. It is rather a *kintsugi* that patches our broken modernity with elements of ancient arts, modern technology, and self-reliance.

A decolonial feminist approach uses principles derived from the exteriorly measurable and deductive worlds as well as the interior, and fertile worlds: from the work of planet preservation; from care professions such as teaching and mothering, rebirthing and creating; from poetry and music; and from making knowledge an active and collective process. A decolonial feminism is explicitly antipatriarchal in nature, meaning the language with which we speak of decolonization must itself be one of reinvention. It is a language in which trauma is healed not only through intellect and struggle but also through arts and poetry, through ancestral knowledge, and through the spiritual nomadism that emanates from African journeys. It is a language that connects people by their peregrinations of body and mind, a language that offers a suture for wounds of the past without neglecting the eternal sentiment at the core of humanity—hope. In short, it needs to be a language of both intellectual and emotional intelligence, a language that helps us to develop an integrity that cannot be compromised from the inside or outside, by any individual or group, by anyone, anywhere.

Which is why this language must avoid excessive jargon. We need to return to speaking straightforwardly about propaganda and brainwashing as much as "epistemic violence." We need to discuss indoctrination along with the "reproduction of colonial aesthetic," and so on. Otherwise, abstract expressions grow more widespread, and fewer people can understand what on earth is being said when they hear talk about decolonizing the mind. If people are confused about what decolonizing the mind means in the first place, then how can they even begin to do it?

By pointing out the limitations of abstract expressions, I do not intend to dismiss it entirely. There is undoubtedly a place for academic debate about decolonization, but *the struggle* for decolonizing the mind is not that place. The language of resistance should not be simplistic or dumbed down, but as bell hooks pointed out in her beautiful essay "Theory as Liberatory Practice," "Any theory that cannot be shared in everyday conversation cannot be used to educate the public."

In 1896 a British delegation looking to control Benin was unexpectedly struck down by the king of Benin, Oba Ovonramwen Nogbaisi. The British retaliated with a barbaric expedition known as the Benin Massacre. A series of plaques at the British Museum's Africa Galleries in London shows British troops looting after the expedition. What makes my heart sink when I look at the elaborate stakes, bows, and rifles of the Beninese on the plaques is their impracticality against the Maxims, rockets, and military technology of the British. What a dignified but misguided effort!

A similar expedition of conquest leads the war to control the mind. Instead of guns and rockets, the colonizer invades the psyche with an artillery of institutionalized and financially backed propaganda. Masculine behavior is superior! American culture is progressive! Climate engineering is the solution! etc. Yet again, we are not equipped with the same machinery. And perhaps that is a good thing. But also, luckily, the mind is not a place where firepower wins. It is a place where clarity wins. As Thiong'o wrote, "Decolonial education is a process of demystifying knowledge and hence reality." I would add that demystifying knowledge is a process of redefining knowledge.

A revolution means to turn something on its head. There are many ways to turn something on its head, but the method that prevents a "re-turn" is to change what is actually inside the head. The feminist cause continues to be neglected, diminished, and co-opted in the conversations about decolonization, but one thing is still as sure as when Sankara said it, "The revolution cannot triumph without the emancipation of women."

of IDENTITY

Waniita mkomunisti
Waniita mkapitalisti
Waniita mnashinalisti
Na mimi ni binadamu tu,
Kwani hilo halitoshi?
They call me communist
They call me capitalist
They call me nationalist
But I am human—
Why is that not enough?

—Alamin Mazrui, "Mimi Ni Mimi (I Am I),"
trans. from Swahili by Katriina Ranne

A people are as healthy and confident as the stories they tell
themselves. Sick storytellers can make nations sick. Without
stories we would go mad. Life would lose its moorings or
orientation . . . stories can conquer fear, you know. They can
make the heart larger.

—Ben Okri

The story begins with a 1612 painting by the leading Baroque artist Peter Paul Rubens now held at the Palazzo Pitti in Florence, Italy. It features four men (including the artist), who sit around a table with a stack of books laid out before them. The men are engaged in a conversation about the works of the Roman philosopher Seneca, whose bust overlooks them. It is titled *The Four Philosophers,* and it conveys precisely the stereotypical image people have of philosophers, namely, that they are of European descent, male, and middle-aged.

Sometimes, in my mind, I replace the image with four black women. It's not because I don't find Rubens's work masterful. It's easy to see why the artwork is so valued. Among other things, it captures with great skill the impulse of intellectual life. But what about the analyses *my* Four Philosophers might make? If a painting of four black women caught in a moment of reflection held the same historical significance and public presence that Rubens's work does, what philosophical seeds would they plant in our collective imagination?

We cannot know because the demographic that shapes the significant discussions are elite European-heritage males. It is their ideas, thoughts, arguments, values, beliefs, attitudes, and preoccupations that dominate our aesthetic, political, cultural, religious, academic, and economic institutions. They are the world's most prominent thinkers, innovators, philosophers, authors, Nobel Prize recipients, and so forth.

European men have contributed profound work; I am not disregarding white men's contributions. Neither am I questioning them solely because they are white and male. That would be to categorically vilify a whole segment of society, which I am unwilling to do not least because I am familiar with its damning consequences.

However, what are the consequences of this monopolization of narrative for other groups? When it comes to identity, what meaning does the concept carry for people who are not white or male? White men are the only demographic who are referred to in standard terms—"doctor," "scientist," "author," and so on. Everyone else is described by a compound word—a "woman doctor," a "black scientist," or an "Asian author." In essence, when we say "author," to stick with the example, we actually mean "white male author" so that an "Asian author" is basically an Asian variant of a white male author.

White males have historically taken possession of "normative identity," which in theory is a "normative identity theft." The consequence is that identity, to the rest of us, becomes a crime scene. The more whiteness and maleness claim "the neutral," "the default," and "the norm," the more marginalized groups—women, people of color, LGBTQ+ communities, Muslims, and other groups whose identities are pushed to the periphery—tend to position their selfhood as ammunition against social inequality. Merely expressing your identity as a black woman or a lesbian or a Muslim or a black lesbian Muslim comes to mean taking up arms in a political struggle.

This politicization of identity is empowering in many ways. It is useful in building community, fostering pride, and repudiating shame. It helps achieve representation in public discourse and popular culture. Consequently, children especially benefit from political declarations of identity as it enables them to see people who are similar to them in the mainstream and to envision their own opportunities. As a proponent of black feminism—an ideology that asserts that people with black and female identities are discriminated against in specific ways—I too am partial to blackness and womanhood.

But if identity is *only* and *automatically* political, it reduces one's humanity to a performance of dissent. Asserting identity becomes an essentialist dramatization, a histrionics of memes. When identity itself becomes ammunition, then the battle is already lost. In such an imbroglio, the abused continue to center the oppressor. They try to persuade him that they too are human. They provide him with facts about the great achievements of women, refugees, lesbians, Muslims, and so on, not to center themselves but to reprimand *him*, retort to *him*, educate *him*, and punish *him*. This exercise leaves them predictably, and perpetually, fatigued and resentful. So the evil cycle continues, leaving little room for joy, the one "weapon" that can truly, if unintentionally, disarm the power of the oppressive narrative.

By *joy*, I am not speaking of its close relative, happiness. I'm referring to an inner quality that is itself political in nature. By *joy*, I mean the type of emotion that may emerge if you had a near-death experience but survived, because to thrive under a system of oppression requires such intentionality. I mean the presence of hope. I mean being yourself even if it clashes with the approved perceptions of how you should be. I mean ease and lightness of being. I mean, in essence, freeing yourself from predefined notions of identity.

An identity that is a vessel of joy does not mean the absence of association with specific groups. Nor does it mean that there isn't a strong sense of self. Personality and identity are conceptually related, but we have misunderstood identity to be the conduit of uniqueness. It is instead personality that ought to inform one's individuality. Living one's identity as a vessel of joy certainly does not mean that there is no despair, anger, and sorrow. It basically means infecting all facets of life—the ups and downs, the political struggles—with willingness to grow, to sit with our frustrations rather than trying to mitigate them.

For a marginalized identity to be a source of joy, it cannot by default exist as an instrument of resistance. Conversely, for an "othered" identity to be a source of resistance, it must be a source of joy. As any abuser knows, the more a victim shares that you've hurt them, the more empowered the abuser becomes. And as any victim of abuse knows, trying to convince someone that you are worthy of respect is not a healthy, joyous way to live.

It takes a tremendous psychological and spiritual effort to tear the internalized story of Europatriarchy to pieces. The centuries-long narrative is so slick and ingrained that to challenge it can feel Sisyphean. From the beginning, the paradigm of Europatriarchal Knowledge dictates what it means to be a girl and a black person and a woman. As Simone de Beauvoir famously said, "One is not born, but rather becomes, a woman." What's worse, it's a becoming that implies suffering.

In some Christian interpretations of the Bible, women were condemned to eternal suffering because of Eve's sins, and black people were damned by the Curse of Ham. It is a tenet of Europatriarchal Knowledge that nonmales, nonwhites, and nonelites live lives of constant dissatisfaction. We are meant to participate in a never-ending inner battle between what our lives are and what we would like them to be. In one way or the other, we were meant to live absent of joy. This is why the biggest "fuck you" a black woman can give to Europatriarchy is to take genuine pleasure in being alive.

Unless a death blow to Europatriarchy saves humanity from the prejudiced way that our identities are politicized, the struggle continues, and joy is, of course, a complicated quality to strive for. Whether it's the African American woman who fears for her children's lives because of police brutality against black children or the South African woman who can't walk safely in her streets for fear of sexual assault or the young black British woman who, despite her talent, faces a lack of opportunities, it can seem impossible. Still, to free black female identity from an apotheosis of suffering, we need to first of all grasp that what we are collectively robbed of is joy and its accompanying sentiments of creativity, hope, ease, security, and freedom.

One day I came across a painting by the artist Mickalene Thomas titled *Le déjeuner sur l'herbe: Les trois femmes noires*. In the piece, three black women gaze confidently at the viewer. I imagine them putting into words their understanding of the underlying meaning of life. The scene has an intimate aura, a slight ambivalence about the world outside—the women are so preoccupied with their own. But there is nevertheless a vague and intangible invitation to conversation with everyone. There is outward-looking in their demeanor; it's all about query, an invitation.

At first I couldn't figure out what was familiar about Thomas's piece. I printed out a copy of it and kept it by my desk for many months. Eventually it hit me like a slam dunk. The women's sensibility was the same as those in Rubens's *Four Philosophers*. I was looking at *the* four philosophers (or rather, three) that I had imagined in my mind's eye.

The title of the work suggests that Thomas was, in fact, presenting her version of another Western classic: Édouard Manet's painting *Le déjeuner sur l'herbe*. But to me, the theme was not merely a luncheon in the grass; it was far more challenging. It was about being and about who has the right to "just be." The women were not asserting their blackness or their womanhood. They were not "other." They were subject.

Rather than viewing identity as a weapon, we should view it as a compass. Like a compass, it helps guide the focus and direction in life. Your woman-compass can help you find distance from men who view women as inferior (if men are your thing). Your black-compass prepares you when an institution you are working with has a legacy of racism. Your class-compass prevents you from feeling shame when you don't have access to the things financially privileged people do. If despite the warnings of your compass, you find yourself in toxic relationships or discriminating situations, it is not a blow to your entire being. You can always reverse and fine-tune your compass so that it can continue to guide you lightly and gently toward the direction of joy. Most significantly, when you look at identity as a compass in this way, you can critique Europatriarchal Knowledge without falling down the pithole of narrowing your own world. To borrow from Toni Morrison, who described the challenges in writing *The Bluest Eye*, "I did the best job I could of describing strategies for grounding my work in race-specific yet race-free prose." The compass makes identity specific yet free.

I've also always loved how Nina Simone described her friendship with playwright and civil rights activist Lorraine Hansberry. "We never talked about men or clothes," she said. "It was always Marx, Lenin, and revolution—real girls' talk." Yet I also like what activist Dick Gregory said about Simone: "There is something about being a woman," he said. "If you look at all the suffering black folks went through, not one black man would dare sing 'Mississippi Goddam.'"

Both examples demonstrate how identity can be a compass rather than a weapon, or as Morrison might say, race specific yet race free (and gender specific yet gender free). In the first instance, Simone and Hansberry challenge the stereotype that women's talk is trivial or male obsessed, while the second statement acknowledges that Simone's black female identity indisputably guided her actions.

Some of my favorite examples of identity as a compass are the letters that the socialist revolutionary Rosa Luxemburg wrote to comrade Sophie Liebknecht, published in *Rosa Luxemburg: or, The Price of Freedom*. Her prison cell was so quiet "that one might as well be already entombed," she wrote, "yet my heart beats with an immeasurable and incomprehensible inner joy."

The power of Luxemburg's words is that, despite that she was writing from a prison cell, they are the words not of an imprisoned mind but of a mind entirely free. They reveal a character to whom identity is expansively liberating rather than confining. In another letter Luxemburg wittily says that she does not identify as a "human being at all but like a bird." She feels more at home "in the meadows when the grass is humming with bees than—at one of our party congresses." How right—a bird has no identity, it doesn't think of itself as a bird, let alone a blue or red bird. Yet despite her flexible relationship with identity, Luxemburg was by no means depoliticized. Even if her "innermost personality belongs more to my tomtits than to the comrades," as she put it, she is clear that she would die for her cause "in a street fight or in prison." As she ultimately did so brutally die for her cause.

Fela Kuti seemed to have discovered a similar quality of political joy free from the narrowing contours of identity during his unwarranted incarceration by the Nigerian state. In his first interview after being released from prison, Kuti was asked, "Do you think your spirit is stronger because of this experience?" to which he replied, "Much more stronger." About whether he was a musician-revolutionary, a kind of "Che Guevara with an orchestra," Fela—who had spent his career pontificating about being an *African man*—responded, "I don't want to say 'call me this.' If you see me strictly as a musician, it's okay. I don't want to say that it is wrong to see me that way. I don't want to say that it is right to see me that way. I want to leave everything to the individual to see me the way they think is right. That's the best way."

In terms of identity, I too don't rigidly define myself this way or that way. I cherish the compasses that my race and gender provide me as a blackwoman. As the words *sunflower*, *breakfast*, or *anybody* mean something entirely different if you separate them, *blackwoman* is in the depths of my mind a compound word with a separate meaning from *black* and *woman*, which I also am. To be a blackwoman has a quality that is understood only by other people who also are black and female. It is a layered yet interthreaded state of identity that you could disentangle only as you would a fluffy ball from a pleat of cotton wool. Softly. But even when separated, the ball of cotton wool is not something else; it is still cotton wool.

I am also African and European. I am mixed race. I am Yoruba. I am Nigerian and Finnish by heritage and Swedish by naturalization. I am a Londoner. I was once a New Yorker. I have varying degrees of affiliation with each of these layers of my identity. I feel at home in Lagos. My roots are embedded in the cultural expressions, sounds, tastes, and rhythms of life that we so easily take for granted until we are distanced from them. I revel in my Finnishness on many occasions, such as when I read Finnish poetry or hike in Finland's beautiful nature. My Finnish identity is marked by nostalgia and melancholy. It's a place I yearn to know better while I also cannot shake off the racism that I attach to my experiences there. My Swedish identity shares a similar quality. However, as I lived in Sweden so many years, I miss it in a more amputated way. Still nowhere in this world is as endearing as London, the city in which I've created what Virginia Woolf called a "room of my own."

Another identity label central to me is feministwriter (again, a compounded and cotton-woolly word). However, even my identity as a feministwriter is one that I have loosened my grip on. Who am I if I'm not a feministwriter? I once wondered. The fact that I had to ponder this question made me realize that I needed a softer relationship to it, as with a compass. Because of my love for both feminism and writing, and the communities they engage me in, I could not afford for these activities to become rigid, self-affirming parts of me, especially in a Europatriarchal world with its insatiability for competitiveness and ranking, hence taking away all the joy from our passions.

More than anything, I come from three countries. First, my body, with its cyclical nature, is a country that doesn't allow me to forget, in the way that men seem to, that I am not above nature. I am a creature of flesh and bones like all mammals. To live in my body is to know both pain and healing, love and grief. Of course, men and women who don't menstruate can have this sense too. But this is one of the reasons that my body informs my sense of self. The second country that I stem from is called my mind. It is a country where patriotism is replaced by contemplation and citizenship by borderlessness. This is where I discover a lagoon of freedom, a small gulf of Minna-ness where any attempts to self-categorize are sedition against the republic. Last, I come from the country of my soul, that undefinable place of stillness, reminiscent of the Hindu concept *namaste,* which expresses a cherishing of both self and every other living being.

Within the space of the body, mind, and soul, my identity is plainly arbitrary. If I were born about half a century earlier, I would still have belonged to the Yoruba and Finno-Karelian tribes. But I would have been British and Russian rather than Nigerian and Finnish, as Nigeria was a British colony and Finland a Russian one. In the countries of body, mind, and soul, my dreams and desires, my grief and my joys, my *human* condition are more important than my race, my gender, my class, my profession.

In *The Spirit of Intimacy*, the Burkinabé writer and teacher Sobonfu Somé wrote that in Dagara knowledge systems, "Each of us is seen as a spirit who has taken the form of a human in order to carry out a purpose. Spirit is the energy that helps us connect, that helps us see beyond our racially limited parameters."

The African approach to identity is commonly a communitarian one, and the community in return is part of the reciprocal physical and spirit realms. The individual is not independent; she is interdependent. Individuality is necessary for ingenuity, so I am critical of the conformity that interdependent approaches to identity can produce, but there is a lot to learn from the shape-shifting and fluid quality given to identity in Africa. Because if we identify with only one thing rather than with *everything*, we subsequently misidentify with whatever values may not be inscribed to our particular identity. For example, men are not supposed to identify with nature except to master it. At a recent gathering, a man told me he'd never buy flowers for himself because "men don't like flowers." If not for the beguilement of power, men would be vociferous about the violent disconnect between masculinity and Mother Nature. I mean, who passionately hates flowers?

Even in the Western world, individual identity is a relatively modern invention, helping encourage consumerism. Every corporation has a target demographic, which requires a conceptualization of identity. In times such as ours, when political consciousness sells, there is massive commodification of progressive movements. Everywhere you can now buy feminist-branded T-shirts, mugs, and so forth. You can basically purchase a ready-made revolutionary identity.

By contrast, an Oxford English Dictionary entry from 1920s

South Africa shared by University of Pittsburgh's Keyword Project shows how much our understanding of identity has changed in just a century. In the entry, the writer contrasts the "policy of subordination" and the "policy of identity" and argues that the policy of identity is flawed since it "refuses to acknowledge any real difference between Europeans and natives." Identity was shunned because it connoted sameness rather than difference, the underpinning concept of apartheid South Africa.

Europatriarchy takes away the poetry of identity. If we look at identity more sensuously, it becomes a commons in which we all have collective ownership. We have created a world in which terms such as *black* and *white*, *woman* and *man* imply specific qualities. How then can we collectively begin to imbue them with different meaning that opens instead of limits? Identity is not something any one person or group can own. Rather, it is a shared quality that enables the human necessity of relationships. Once social relationships change, society changes because society is made of social relations.

There is a fragility to identity. It's like being an egg on a crate. The platform in which the egg stands is reliable and firm, as shared humanity is, but the egg itself is fragile as identity can be. To focus on the crate rather than the egg is not to diminish the force of life and nourishment within each egg but to see that the real support comes from the foundation of being human first.

of BLACKNESS

*What, then, is a race? It is a vast family of human beings,
generally of common blood and language, always of common
history, traditions, and impulses, who are both voluntarily
and involuntarily striving together for the accomplishment of
certain more or less vividly conceived ideals of life.*

—W. E. B. Du Bois

"I love to be black" reads the last sentence in my journal entry of
May 31, 1993. I was going on fifteen. I wrote the passage a couple
of years after moving to Sweden from Nigeria, where I'd spent
my childhood. It was likely the first time I'd reflected on blackness
and on the racial prejudice I was experiencing in my new home-
town, Malmö. A few journal pages later, there are three separate
clauses on an otherwise blank page,

Black is beautiful.
Black Power rules the continent.
The word black means: Pride, Beauty, Intelligent [*sic*].

It was while working on this chapter that I searched through
old journals for clues of when I first began to identify as black. I
knew that it wasn't growing up in Nigeria, for if I identified with

any "color" then, it would have been yellow. I never did identify as yellow, but people referred to my complexion with the term. This habit originates with the Yoruba term *pupa*, translated into English as "yellow" but in actuality referring to the entire ocherous range—anything orangey, reddish, or tannish is *pupa*. To be called yellow was either a compliment to suggest exotic looks or an insult implying naivete. Children would sing.

> *Pawpaw is a kind of fruit*
> *Sweet like sugar, yellow like Fanta,*
> *Everybody likes pawpaw*

It reflected the duality that to be yellow is to be sweet, like pawpaw (papaya), which "everybody likes," but alternatively that you're too sweet for your own good.

Although Nigerians generally had an awareness of and felt an affinity with the term *black* on a global and historical scale, it was not how we identified in a national context. This lack of association with the word *black* may seem understandable. To identify as black within Nigeria—the world's largest black nation—appears inessential.

But it *is* essential. Although blackness isn't a concept that should be taken to rigidly describe ethnic or national belonging, it is of central importance also within Africa because it binds together Africa's descendants sociohistorically (involving social and historical factors). For people of black African heritage, this sociohistorical context is the glue that connects us. For all intents and purposes, blackness *is* a sociohistorical context.

Yet my journal entry reveals that "becoming black" was marked by two factors none of which were to do with this sociohistorical context. First, I grew up in Nigeria, where blackness was not an influential concept. Second, I came of age in Sweden, where blackness was a cause of blatant discrimination. It was not enough to state that I loved to be black; I accompanied my journal declaration with clarifications: "I love to be black [because] black is powerful, proud, beautiful, intelligent." A key element in my becoming consciously black was clearly to resist the Europatriarchal definitions that claimed otherwise—that blackness was powerless, shameful, ugly, and unintelligent. In other words, rather than with the rich legacies of African heritage people, blackness came with an inherent protest, a need to object to erroneous definitions of blackness and to defiantly assert positive, empowering ones.

The need to affirm one's blackness manifests uniquely from individual to individual and group to group. But oppression, defiance, and protest (against white supremacy) are today seen as tantamount to blackness. One is not born, but rather one becomes, black, to extrapolate from Simone de Beauvoir's saying, "One is not born, but rather becomes, a woman."

Consider Nina Simone's anthem-like song "To Be Young, Gifted and Black," where she sings that to be young, gifted and black is "where it's at," as these qualities in themselves evoke pride.

The word *black* here is doing something similar to what I did in my journal entries. It is indirectly repudiating negative definitions of blackness by affixing an empowering message to it instead. Simone captures completely this reciprocal process of resistance and reaffirmation in her performance of the song at Morehouse College in Atlanta in 1969. At the end of the mighty show, as the camera glazes over the audience, you can almost touch their rebuke to racist notions of blackness and their corresponding awakening of pride. If you weren't black before you went into this show, you sure were black when you came out of it. Indeed, Simone dedicated the song to the black lesbian feminist playwright Lorraine Hansberry, Simone's mentor, after whose play the song is titled. Simone said, "Lorraine started off my political education, and through her I started thinking about myself as a black person in a country run by white people and a woman in a world run by men."

If blackness is a political identity to African descendants in the diaspora, on the African continent there is a hesitation to engage fully with the concept precisely therefore. We have more than enough to grapple with—ethnic rivalry, religious division, sycophantic leadership, arch-patriarchy, and imperial exploitation, to name a few. Maybe blackness, packed with its political baggage, is one thing we can forget about?

I think there is more to the story. We don't fully embrace blackness because where roles were once reversed, there is a growing sense of superiority in being African rather than black. There is a pride about the rich ethnic heritage and culture in Africa, and rightly so, but that heritage and culture belong to all people of African descent: Yoruba, Hausa, Igbo, Mende, Zulu, Swahili, Fulani, Bambara, Mandinka, Tigrinya, and Tutsi, even those whose ability to trace their ethnic lineage was disrupted by the transatlantic slave trade.

The term *Africa* is a colonial invention not used by black people until the eighteenth century when authors and activists like Ignatius Sancho and Phillis Wheatley began to present themselves as African, partly to propagate Christianity, as historian James Sidbury writes in "Becoming African in America." The word *black*, on the other hand, is older than our understanding of ourselves as African. African history is the history of black people and not vice versa. The mere fact that we still have to differentiate "sub-Saharan Africa" (previously "Black Africa") speaks to the fact that the term *Africa* in itself is not synonymous with *black*.

The word *Africa*, it is widely believed, originated in the word *Ifriqiya*, formerly the name used for North Africa or, more precisely, the coastal regions of what today are western Libya, Tunisia, and eastern Algeria, which once formed the Roman province of Africa (Ifriqiya). Sub-Saharan Africa was referred to separately then, as it still is now.

It had multiple names, and all of them had to do with blackness. For example, *Aethiopia*, the word that once referred to all of black Africa, means "black" or, literally, "sunburned" in ancient Greek. Similarly, *Bilad as-Sudan*, as the Arabs called black Africa, means "the land of the blacks." One of the first known human civilizations, the ancient Egyptians, called their civilization *Kemet*, which means "the black land." *Mauritania*, another term that once meant black Africa, stems from *maurus*, "black" in Latin, and informs *Moor*. Herodotus, the "father of history" (484–425 BCE), wrote about the "Nasamonians," which is believed to mean "Negroes of Ammon." Nubia was the land of a dark-skinned people, and one of the world's oldest civilizations, the Iron Age Nok culture, established around 1500 BCE, the Iron Age Nok culture, located in present-day Nigeria, is believed to owe its name to blackness. The term *black* is itself one of the world's twenty-three "ultraconserved words," meaning humanity's oldest words, which have meant mainly the same thing in several language groups for over fifteen millennia. I am not suggesting that these terms had the racial connotation we associate with blackness today. My point instead is that blackness has a long history that goes beyond the modern racial hierarchy system or nationalistic borders. As long as we see ourselves only as African, and not black, we will neglect the framing of continuity between history and the present; diaspora and continent.

There is a hip-hop tradition where emcees come together in

a circle known as a cypher to share their rhymes in turns. The cypher traveled from various locations in Africa to the diaspora. The same structure is present in the *roda de samba* (Samba circles) of Brazil, where participants take turns entering the center to dance, or the Haitian Vodun ritual, where dance is a meditation to ecstasy.

In the cypher, everyone brings their unique rhymes and styles, and each emcee is cheered on by the others. Participants are aware that, while there may be playful competitiveness, the variety of styles and voices only enriches the cypher as a whole.

There is a call-and-response element present in the cypher. The combination of verbal and nonverbal communications— words, dance, martial arts, trance, and performance—is used toward a goal, and that is to teach and transform.

Blackness is a cypher where the conversation is intergenerational, international, and interdependent. The West African talking drums are precursors to calypso, which is a precursor to hip-hop. Where talking drums (a traditional African technology used to mimic human speech) relay proverbs, we hear poetry in rap. Where there is boasting in rap, there are panegyrics in the talking drums. When a rapper samples, she is evoking the role of the griot, passing ancient knowledge to a new audience.

In the 1800s enslaved Africans in the Caribbean already had developed calypso as a means of documenting their history and providing sociopolitical commentary. The word *calypso* comes from the Efik (eastern Nigerian language) word *kaiso*, meaning "go on." Here too we see the polyphonic roots of the talking drums embedded in a new type of Sensuous Knowledge. The talking drums were not primitive instruments, as Europatriarchal Knowledge made them out to be. They remain a multilayered grammar that includes a feminine and a masculine drum language as well as grammatical tenses. We miss the frame of history that blackness provides when our entire focus is on its political meaning.

The point is not to assert that blackness isn't at all political. Hardly. But we emphasize political blackness to the detriment of what blackness also should conjure—the history, the knowledge, the stories, the epics, the civilizations—basically, the collective memory—of black people themselves and not only their painful encounters with whiteness. As bell hooks says in "Postmodern Blackness," "It has become necessary to find new avenues for transmitting the messages of black liberation struggle, new ways to talk about racism and other politics of domination." It is not only black people who remain oppressed by Europatriarchy; blackness itself—as a concept—is unfree.

A few years ago, I was invited to give a talk at a literary festival in Cachoeira, an enchanting small town in Brazil's largest black state, Bahia. During my trip, I visited the first cemetery for black people in the country. I wondered where black people were buried before then, feeling my heart pierced when I conjured the answers to that question. I had read that enslaved Africans in the US would bury their loved ones facing the west—toward Africa. I took solace in noting that if they cast the dead into the sea behind the cemetery, it pointed homeward.

For enslaved Africans, *homeward* would have been a noun, not an adverb. It would be a country, not an orientation. It would be the last place from which their journey to the diasporas began. Homeward would be a place like Badagry, the beach that my family and I frequently visited when I was a child. But it was also the major slave-trading port where Europeans abducted hundreds of thousands of people and enslaved them.

Badagry, with the connotations it harbors, is ever present in my awareness. I can never stop thinking about Badagry, needing to visit Badagry, seeking to make sense of Badagry. A part of my psyche cannot reconcile those leisurely family resorts Badagry was known for with the people ambushed and sent into the great unknown from there.

In Lagos, I find myself longing for landmarks that house the ghosts of Homeward and announce the importance of this disastrous event in history, but they are absent. I feel the need to visit a place that doesn't exist. I need a place to mourn, honor, and reflect with others who also yearn to acknowledge consciously the wounds of history.

"Poetry is the place of transcendence," bell hooks says in *Wounds of Passion*. It is true that if we transcend, it will be because we satisfy the urgent need for reflection in Nigeria. We need cultural monuments, museums, and memorials that weave the legacy of slavery and colonialism into the national mythology. Our collective imagination should be shaped by cultural interventions that express the confluence of ambitions that created Nigeria in the first place. How healing it would be to visit modern shrines that honor the gods of retrospection. Sadly, the reluctance of Nigerians to engage with blackness is one of the reasons such sites do not exist. My point is not that we should diminish our African pride. Rather, it is that it is only if we engage with blackness too, that we will begin to connect the dots of history and the present.

Conversely, without a widespread emphasis on the African context of blackness, the black diaspora more and more fails to connect the struggle against white supremacy with that against the militarily capitalist exploitation of the African continent. Time and again, artists, writers, and activists in the diaspora neglect to connect the black struggle against police brutality or poverty in black communities or prejudice in the West with African realities. Conscious hip-hop in the US, for example, often provides biting commentary on racism in law enforcement but rarely discusses the relationship between US law enforcement and US military bases in Africa. Similarly, for all the radical actions of the Black Lives Matter movement, the failure to tie it together with pan-African and anti-imperialist struggle beyond rhetoric is a missed opportunity.

Blackness instead centers on resistance to white supremacy, which limits people's understanding of blackness as a sociohistorical reality. Blackness remains scarred by what W. E. B. Du Bois described as "double consciousness," that "sense of measuring one's soul by the tape of a world that looks on in amused contempt and pity." Blackness also remains shaped by something writer James Baldwin said in his essay "Princes and Powers" that "all black men held in common," namely, "their unutterably painful relation to the white world." And Martin Luther King, another great avatar of blackness, explained his heated and controversial opposition to the slogan "Black Power" in his autobiography by writing, "Beneath all the satisfaction of a gratifying slogan, Black Power was a nihilistic philosophy born out of the conviction that the Negro can't win."

We continue to view blackness not merely as a condition of being but also as a *contention* of being. For blackness to be liberating, it needs to move away from automatically signifying "contention." I don't mean that we should ignore the gross immorality and wicked injustice of white supremacy. Or that we should overlook the structural crimes that continue to affect black people everywhere because of white supremacist legacies. We should fight the effects of racism to the bitter end, but if anything that fight needs to be framed by its culprit, whiteness. It is whiteness, not blackness, that transmits a history of racism.

We teach black children about racism from a young age while

white children (who at best will benefit from the privilege of racist systems and at worst will perpetuate them) can reach adulthood before learning about race. As the words of Du Bois, Baldwin, and King hint at, blackness should offer a conceptual space of freedom; of reconfiguration, revelation, and revolution. We should primarily teach black children that blackness connotes a sensibility beyond nation, ethnicity, or generation. Blackness is a transmitter of shared history, ancestry, lineage, and belonging. Blackness is a repository of a people's philosophy and of folklore and epics that convey collective attitudes to fundamental matters of life such as birth, death, love, work, and pleasure. We need to free blackness from the semantic burden of continually producing a language of dissent while not concurrently producing one of joy.

In 2017, I found myself on the same flight to Lagos as the fifty-first *Ooni* (king) of Yorubaland, Ooni Adeyeye Enitan Babatunde Ogunwusi. In the hope of adding primary research to my yearslong engagement with Yoruba thought, I immediately—and admittedly somewhat opportunistically—took the chance to introduce myself to the highest spiritual leader and most influential monarch of millions of black people in Nigeria and the diaspora.

A few weeks later, I found myself at the palace in Ile-Ife, the city where the Ooni resides and which to the Yoruba represents the cradle of civilization. Experiencing the rituals, the processions, the customs, the history, and the traditions and, memorably, receiving a personal reading from the Ooni during which he blessed the ensuing efforts of this book, I was reminded of the spirit of cosmopolitanism inherent in Yoruba culture. I grew up aware that my own ethnic heritage, Yoruba, was tolerant and embracing of difference, but my visit to the Ooni's palace reinvigorated the awareness.

During my visit, members of the US consulate arrived to speak with the Ooni of Ife. They wanted to arrange a cultural program in Ife, as so many Americans of African heritage visit the town yearly. The meeting took place in a large and crowded hall with a theatrical display of concentrated status. Once everyone settled, the Ooni looked the US consulate staff—three white men—in the eyes and said, with compassion, "Welcome home."

The men blushed uncomfortably. The Ooni chuckled, "You may not understand that this is your home, but Ife is the home of all humanity. It is the cradle of civilization." The Ooni continued, "Everybody originates from the black man, and the black man originates from Ife. At the beginning of time, humans lived here because the best place for human survival is tropical Africa. The family tree of all of humanity leads back here."

Intrigued, I noted to myself that this attitude is both our doom and our salvation. We humble-brag, you could say—welcome you like a family member but simultaneously let you know that, rest assured, "ours" is the cradle of humankind. We are proudly attached to what is ours, but we also give it away too easily, given the acquisitive intentions that often accompany foreign interests.

Later that same evening, a large number of mainly African American and some Caribbean musicians arrived at the palace. We all gathered in one of the palace's rooms for another ceremony. The Ooni delivered the same talk to them, with the same warmth. But this audience did not blush, they gushed. They *were* home, and they *were* the proprietors of Ife. There was nothing to resist in this message but everything to embrace. At that moment in time, everybody in the room was connected by a powerful, unnamed energy that immersed the room with a feeling of reciprocal kinship. This is what blackness is, I thought. *This* story, which connects black people from Nigeria to the US to Brazil to Haiti to Cuba. *This* mutual sentiment, which binds us socially and historically.

At the time of my visit, it was public knowledge that the Ooni was searching for a wife. He and his previous wife had split, and it wasn't kosher for someone of his rank to remain unmarried. A friend half-jokingly warned me that it would be a cultural violation to reject such a proposal should one be made.

I was not naive enough to imagine that the Ooni would not assess my potential suitability for this role. And nor was I innocent enough to not be respectfully flirtatious. I say "respectfully," as it was not exactly a situation where one could openly flirt. I had to observe protocol such as to refer to him as "Kabiyesi" (Your Highness); a title I would normally refrain from when flirting. Yet, although our WhatsApp correspondence centered on my research, we enjoyed a mutual rapport. During my stay at the palace, we stayed up until the early hours sharing a stimulating conversation about our mutual interests in philosophy, meditation, and history. He made sure that I was treated exceptionally well, and he treated his staff and guests with courtesy. I came to see in him a kindness, which to me is an attractive quality in a man. Were he a guy who lived around the block, and not the flipping Ooni of Ife, I would have enjoyed seeing him again.

As it was, the mere fantasy, however farfetched, of life in the palace as the first *feminist* Olori (Queen) of Yorubaland was, despite its revolutionary feminist allure, exasperating. Everywhere the Ooni went—in fact, any time he rose from or sank into his seat—there was a procession, a ritual, a song, bells ringing, a never-ending tribute to the notions of divinity, authority, and royalty. As someone wary of authoritarian thinking and the idea of a messiah of any kind, I was exhausted by all the pomp and ceremony. I pondered how the Ooni coped with this spectacle, especially since before becoming Ooni, he was indeed the guy around the block. It turns out he lived not too far from my house in Lagos.

Nevertheless, it was one of the most meaningful journeys of my life, perhaps the closest a nonreligious person can get to a spiritual pilgrimage. Witnessing the cosmopolitan spirit of blackness—afropolitanism—was one of the reasons that made it so.

As I was writing this chapter, a song kept repeating in my mind. It was *"Rivers of Babylon"* by the Rastafarian group the Melodians. It took me a while before I recognized why. The song captures the struggle of black people perfectly, but it also points to the delicate quandary that we have yet to respond to.

In the biblical tale from which the song is adapted (Psalm 137:1–4 in the Hebrew Bible), it was the Jews who were forced into exile from Zion to Babylon. For Rastafarians, "Babylon" represents the exploitative spirit of the West while "Zion" refers broadly to Ethiopia, which historically referred to the homeland of all black people, Africa. "King Alpha" refers to Haile Selassie, the Ethiopian leader whom Rastafarians believe was a messiah and whose reference caused the song to be initially banned in Jamaica as it replaced "The Lord's song" with "King Alpha song."

The question at the song's heart—"How can we sing King Alpha song in a strange land?"—is what Africa's black descendants have been asking in different ways, with different languages, in different places, for centuries. It is the question at the center of the revolt of enslaved people in the Americas, in the independence struggles in Africa, in the modern-day movements to end racism in the US, Brazil, South Africa, Israel, Sweden, India, and the UK. The entire black struggle expresses the yearning conveyed in that one question, which you could translate,

Oh, how shall we sing of freedom under oppression?
How shall the children of Africa sing of liberation
when their home imprisons them?
How can the daughters and sons of Africa not only survive
but thrive given the circumstances of history?

It remains the most critical question to answer.

One of the ways to sing the "King Alpha song in a strange land" is with the sociohistorical context of blackness as the harmony. We can and should be proud of our ethnicity and nationality, but as grammar is the glue that connects words into sentences, paragraphs, and chapters, so is blackness the harmony that gels the past, present, and the future of African heritage people into a "King Alpha Song."

of WOMANHOOD

Waxing Gibbous

Blue is a feminine color in Africa.

According to the ancient myths, this is because Goddess Asi of the Foya Kamara in modern-day Sierra Leone yearned to possess the blue color of the sky, the lakes, and the birds of paradise, whose feathers were dyed so brightly blue she had to squint to look at them. One day, despite the consequences of using her powers for personal yearnings, Asi prepared a ritual so that the spirits would grant her the sublime color that occupied her thoughts.

She tucked her newborn baby into a white *lappa* cloth, strapped her around her back, and walked down to the banks of the River Niger to prepare a fire. Once the flames danced, Asi took off the *lappa* and lay her daughter some distance away from the heat. She began the ritual, chanting and dancing in the shape of the flames. Eventually, the fire stilled down, and so did Asi. When all that remained were ashes, Asi rubbed her body with the dust. She knew that her request was received. All she needed to do was to wait for the color blue to appear to her in some special manner. She decided to return the next day.

Asi went to pick up her baby, but the *lappa* she had been ensconced in was empty. All that remained under the rectangular piece of white cloth was the pillow of leaves she had gathered from the vines to cushion the child. Asi let out a long wail, realizing at once that the gods had punished her for the ritual by taking her baby away. She held the leaves against her chest and sobbed feverishly, which covered her body in a mix of ashes, leaves, and salty tears.

Once she began to awaken to reality, Asi wiped the mucky liquid off her body with the *lappa* cloth. It was then that she saw a deep blue stain appear on the fabric. That was how Asi discovered that when you mix indigo leaves with salt, liquid, and ashes, it produces the color blue. She had paid a heavy price for the discovery.

"Please give me my baby back!" Asi screamed. The spirits responded, "You will conceive a different baby with the same soul, but on one condition." Asi listened as the spirits said, "You may only share the knowledge of how to extract the color blue from the indigo plant with women."

First Quarter

From the River Niger to the River Nile, women were the proprietors of the color blue in Africa. Like Goddess Asi, the people of Kemet, or ancient Egypt, coveted the color blue so much that they went on dangerous expeditions to the Sinai and the Sar-i Sang mines in Afghanistan, home of the lapis lazuli stone, to acquire some of the gold-freckled blue stone, which they called *khesbedj*.

Khesbedj was used to make jewelry, decorations, and cosmetics. It resembled a starry night sky, so it was also used to honor the sky goddess Nut (pronounced "Newht"). In almost all ancient cultures, sky gods are male while earth goddesses are female. But in Kemet the roles were reversed; Nut was the goddess of the sky while Geb was the god of the earth.

Centuries later, Kemetians invented the world's first synthetic color, known today as Egyptian blue. They assigned it to another goddess, Wadjet, whose symbol, the blue-tinted Eye of Horus, became an amulet of protection against evil forces.

Belief in goddesses such as Nut and Wadjet explains why womanhood in Kemet was respected more than it was in other civilizations. However, respect and equality are not the same thing. Kemet too was a patriarchal civilization. Royal and noble women may have had access to power, but men as a social group governed women.

However, in the Eighteenth Dynasty, Queen Hatshepsut, upon the death of her husband, King Thutmose II, defied tradition and declared herself heir to the throne. She ruled as pharaoh for twenty-two years between 1490 and 1468 BCE and brought great wealth to the dynasty. She reestablished trade with foreign countries such as the Land of Punt and raided Sinai and led military expeditions to Canaan and Nubia.

What is particularly interesting about Hatshepsut, however, is her refusal to appropriate typical attributes of masculinity to establish power. She complemented her firm hand with a penchant for beauty; she imported exotic plants and commissioned hundreds of architectural projects in Kemet that would not be rivaled by any other culture for many centuries. It was Hatshepsut who ordered the creation of a significant number of the Kemetian statues found in the world's museums today.

These are probably the reasons why her successor, Thutmose III, upon her death, ordered her *damnatio memoriae* (erased from history). All Hatshepsut's monuments, her sphinxes and tablets, were demolished and expunged in an attempt to wipe her name out of the records. It was not until the middle of the nineteenth century, when archaeologists rediscovered her tomb, that the story of the great ruler began to emerge.

The attempted erasure of Hatshepsut from history books was probably no accident. Ancient Egyptians retained the remnants of *Queen* Hatshepsut's legacy. It is only the statuaries and engravings of her as pharaoh, as *King* Hatshepsut, that were demolished.

In other words, we can trace to Kemet not only the association of the color blue with womanhood in Africa but also the origins of patriarchy in Africa.

Waxing Crescent

Similar excavations of women mark the history of the continent. The highest spiritual throne of the Yoruba civilization, the Ooni of Ife, has held a woman only once out of fifty-one reigns. That woman was the twenty-first Ooni, Luwoo. She too ruled Ife, the first city of Yorubaland, with rigor; she too beautified the city more than others before her. She also was the cause of so much hostility that after her reign, the kings decided that no other woman would retake the position.

Comparably, women's participation in guerrilla warfare campaigns against colonial powers in countries such as Angola, Mozambique, Guinea, and Algeria was repressed after independence, and it was as though women had not taken part at all.

The same is true of the black liberation struggle at large. We hear of the great deeds of men such as Kwame Nkrumah, Malcolm X, Bantu Stephen Biko, Frantz Fanon, Wole Soyinka, Nelson Mandela, George Padmore, Walter Rodney, Patrice Lumumba, and Marcus Garvey. We don't hear about the equally important work of Charlotte Maxeke, a committed organizer of women's and workers' rights in South Africa, or Amy Ashwood Garvey, the Jamaican Pan-Africanist who created connections between the diaspora. Or Adelaide Casely-Hayford, the Sierra Leonean author and speaker who traveled the world advocating for educational justice, or Elaine Brown, who led the Black Panther Party from 1974 to 1977.

In her thrilling memoir *A Taste of Power*, Elaine Brown writes that she eventually left the party because "I would not tolerate any raised fists in my face or any Black Power handshakes, or even the phrase 'Black Power,' for all of it now symbolized to me the denial of black women in favor of the freedom of 'the black man.'"

It's the same story over and over again. Female leaders are silenced when it comes to power. As Rabiaa Nejlaoui, a Tunisian parliamentarian, says in a documentary by FEMNET, an African organization promoting women's development, "Men think that politics is not the field of women. They think that this field is theirs. It's like they own it."

Truth be told, politics, as it plays out today, *is* owned by men. For women to make it our field, we will need to change not only how politics is shaped but also how politics is defined in the first place.

New Moon

According to Yoruba custom, if you feed a baby a pinch of the following seven food items at their naming ceremony, they will fare well in life. Water (*omi*) is given because everything everlasting in life needs water to survive. Palm oil (*epo*) with its lubricant quality enables a smooth flow in life. The kola nut (*obi*), which is initially bitter but sweetens as it is chewed on, is a reminder that some of the sweetest things in life are bitter at first. Honey (*oyin*) is given for a balmy and "golden" life. Pepper (*ata*) is given to ensure the right dose of toughness, and salt (*iyo*) for a deliciously delectable experience. As for dried fish (*eja*), they are a reminder that, like fish, we must continue to swim no matter how rough the waters may be.

It was my grandmother, Alhaja Aduke Salami, who placed a pinch of *omi, epo, obi, oyin, ata, iyo,* and *eja* on my tongue at my naming ceremony. The Awon Ifa, as the ritual is called, would not be the last time she had me consume traditional herbs and medicinal foods. Long into my childhood, my grandmother would give my cousins and me herbal mixtures known as *agbo*, often in secrecy from my grandfather, who with his Western, Christian education thought of the (admittedly repulsive) concoctions as sinful.

My grandmother lived alternatingly in the same house that my parents, aunts, uncles, cousins, and I also did. By profession, she was an *iya oloja*, a chief market woman. She made and sold *Adire*, a fabric on which apotropaic patterns (to repel harmful influences) are made with raffia threads and then dyed in indigo pots to produce a batik pattern. It was a tradition she learned from her mother, who learned it from her mother, who learned it from her mother, who as the myth goes, learned somewhere down the line from the Great Mother, Asi.

Everything I loved resided in Lagos—my parents, my large extended family, my closest friends, sunshine, hibiscus, talking drums, mangoes, you name it. I was aware of the horrors that took place in my city. Only the most sheltered Lagosians could claim ignorance of them. Any given morning on my way to school, I might see people being burned to death for accusations of theft, or I'd see a dead body by the side of a road, or we'd have riots in school. Once I came home from school, it was often to a home without electricity or water. When my mother and I sat outside on the balcony in the evenings, I understood that it was not *really* because of the beauty of the dark blue starry night sky, as she suggested, but rather because to stay indoors with no electricity or water would mean prickly, suffocating heat. Yet those nights under the dark blue starry sky (Nut, hello?) were precious to me. "Can you see that star watching over us?" my mother would ask me and point at the brightest star she could spot. "Yes," I would respond. "It's Minna-Mummo," Finnish for "Grandmother Minna".

My Nigerian grandmother performed the ritual of my naming ceremony, but it was my Finnish great-grandmother, Minna Tuomaala, for whom I was named. *Those* two factors—my baptism by my Nigerian grandmother into the name of my Finnish great-grandmother—gathered themselves together into one big star that to me represented the essence of female ancestry against the backdrop of the indigo sky.

Sometimes, in the early evenings just after sunset when the heat dissipated and just before night when scourges of mosquitoes filled the air, I would join my grandmother on the patio watching as she stirred and salted pieces of cloth as though she were making soup. Watching her transform transparent material into deep velvet blue, I entered a world of craftswomen and African feminine knowledge systems that were not available to me in my otherwise patriarchal, colonized, and rough city setting in Lagos.

It was during these formative years in Nigeria that my feminist consciousness developed. All the women in the family compound contributed. First of all my mother—there is not a thing that enriches my life today that I don't have her to thank for. "Never compromise your happiness": this was her message to me from as far back as I can remember. Our house help, Margaret, a second mother of sorts to me and a woman who was sharp, fierce, and empowered in ways that few middle- to upper-class Nigerian women were, thanks to their colonial education and religious indoctrination. My aunties, who stood tall despite the shenanigans of the men around them. My grandmother, who preserved the old feminine traditions of ritual, herbalism, and Adire making with a self-assurance typical of her generation of African women.

There were connections between all of these worlds. I understood subconsciously that Adire was a status symbol, an expression of ancestral pride and social commentary. I knew it could also be worn as a prayer, like Wadjet's Eye of Horus. The Adire fabric named "Olokun" (the goddess of the sea in the Yoruba pantheon of gods), for example, consists of twenty-eight different patterns, each representing a proverb attributed to the goddess.

However, I understood also that it was pink, and not blue, that I was supposed to be fascinated with. It was pink that girls were socialized to associate with the state of womanhood that we so desperately wished for. It was pink that was connected to those branded American figurines with plastic smiles, perky breasts, and bendable pointy feet. It was therefore pink that I dutifully embraced as a feminine color. But Barbie and her pink weapons won only a pyrrhic victory, for in my heart I yearned for the depth and mystery of the color blue.

Waning Crescent

A few months before my thirteenth birthday—and the teenage years I looked forward to spending with my best friends in Nigeria—my mother and I moved to Sweden, as a military coup had made life in Nigeria even more politically and economically challenging than it already was. We were lucky to have the opportunity to escape, unlike most Nigerians. But although life in Sweden would eventually hold many positives, I was devastated. I missed Nigeria and my father, although he visited as frequently as he could. I could not speak Swedish and found it hard to make friends. I was bullied and physically attacked because of my skin color.

And yet the worst was to come: I got my period. It was not the physiological development of menstruation that depressed me; it was the symbolic meaning. Starting my period signified that I was becoming a woman, and that prospect seemed uninviting, as it was clear to me by then that women were unhappy with the predicament of being women. After all, they always complained about their husbands, their bodies, their lack of opportunities—basically, their lot in life.

However, I was enraptured by some women. Those in magazines and movies—they were bold, free, and playful, as I wanted to be. But "real" women, the ones that I knew and that I observed, were what the philosopher and activist Noam Chomsky in the book *On Western Terrorism* called the "unpeople" (a term he borrowed from the wise ancestor George Orwell).

Chomsky argued that the motive of what he called "intellectual and moral colonization" is to "get the unpeople to accept that it [oppression] is natural." He gave the example of how women, for millennia, accepted being the property of their husbands and fathers because they had internalized the patriarchal education that told them that it was women's role to serve others and to have no rights themselves. Simply put, the unpeople are those who for diverse reasons are complicit in their own oppression.

The ways that women are made the unpeople today have thankfully decreased. Since Saudi Arabia legalized women's suffrage in 2015, there is no country where women can't vote, and women everywhere are securing new freedoms and rights.

Still, in many parts of the world, women remain the possessions of their husbands, fathers, and patriarchal culture at large. Even among modern, educated women in Nigeria, many wives still ask their husbands' permission for basic things such as doing the work they'd like to do or going out with friends or even spending time with their birth families.

Everywhere around the globe, women still accept and protect patriarchy in myriad ways—by executing traditions that harm women's bodies or by carrying out unpaid labor within the domestic space or by taking men's family names or through worshipping male gods or by supporting imperialism or through heedlessly raising entitled boys who continue to oppress future generations of women.

These are only some of the ways that women are patriarchal, and it is no accident that they are. Men know that the best way to dominate women is to manipulate them into oppressing themselves so that *they* don't have to. Male supremacists have always used culture, religion, tradition, politics, education, psychological tactics, and violence to force women to think patriarchally. Practices such as breast ironing, female genital mutilation, and widow punishment are often carried out by women themselves. Women are socialized to uphold denigrating views about women's roles in the family, in politics, in sexual life, and in society at large. Even those many women who hate patriarchy often have no choice but to succumb to its demands because of their social and financial position.

Detrimental as structural oppressions are, the ultimate weapon in turning women against women is the Europatriarchal nature of knowledge production itself. If our approach to knowledge production is patriarchal, then ultimately everything we know, and everything we do as a result of what we know, will be patriarchal too. If knowledge production is systemically antiwoman, then these values will shape everything from our intimate relationships to our social structures.

It is in those deep recesses of ingrained psychological and social behavior that seeds for lasting change can also be planted.

Moreover, because those interior places are indeed especially affected by poetics, creativity, and imagination, to rescue womanhood from the "unpeople" position it has held for too long, we deleteriously negate the imaginative—playing, exploring patterns, using mixed methodologies such as stories, sound, or embodied analysis and synthesis—that has always constituted women's ways of knowing in favour of administrative and bureaucratic indexes and statistics.

Within this psychosocial context, I contend that women are patriarchal because adulthood is, by default, constructed as manhood, and so becoming an adult when you are female means appropriating manhood. By *adulthood* I don't in this instance mean attaining a legal age, buying a house, having a pension fund, or other signifiers of the responsibilities that come with being a grown-up. Instead I am reflecting on adulthood as it relates to the more complex behavioral sense of *personhood*, which involves feelings of independence, self-worth, strength, fearlessness, clarity of thought, responsibility, and most of all, self-reliance.

Likewise, by *manhood*, I mean not maleness per se but rather the value system that is constructed around men and masculinity. Since the psychosocial conditioning of manhood contains an abundant element of sexism—that is, the reduction, repudiation, and resentment of that which represents the feminine—when a woman transitions toward adulthood and begins to appropriate conditioned male psychology (being that adulthood is equated with manhood), she simultaneously enters a landscape of self-loathing. This was why my becoming a woman terrified me. I was standing on the threshold of what I perceived to be a threat to my sense of self-worth.

My fears were justified. If indeed adulthood is psychosocially defined by manhood, then womanhood, if it can be psychosocially defined by any one thing at all, is defined by a lack of maleness.

Whether this manifests as the lack of a boy child, a husband, *or* attributes that will gain the approval of men, such as a specific look and body type, a humble demeanor, and so forth, a woman is always chasing something that she perceives to be essential to her very womanhood but that in reality is necessary to her proximity to manhood.

This is why, if and when women attain the deep sense of independence and self-reliance that form personhood, which for many women is in later life—say, after a divorce, when they find themselves asking for the first time what *they* really want out of life—their new attitude is invariably associated with manhood. They are told that they act or think "like a man." A woman who "acts like a woman" implies a woman who upholds accepted submissive, self-deprecating norms. We have to wonder why, when boys are being raised to attain personhood from childhood, we haven't insisted on the same for our daughters. Until little girls can proudly grow into women who "act like women" when they are being self-assured and autonomous as much as when they are being compassionate or emotional, then feminist work is incomplete.

Third Quarter

In Frantz Fanon's *Black Skin, White Masks*, he writes, "At the risk of arousing the resentment of my colored brother, I will say that the black man is not a man." He proceeds to explain that the black man is a man only insofar as he can compare with, compete with, or strive to be a white man—that what we know to be the black man depends on what we know to be the white man.

What I am arguing about womanhood is similar. A woman is

an adult, in the sense of personhood described earlier, only insofar as she can compare with, compete with, strive to be, or in the case of heterosexual women also *secure* a man.

Like Fanon, I too risk offending my sisters by arguing that what we know to be a woman depends on what we know to be a man. From the second a girl is born, she is called to identify and relate to her life through male psychology. She gets her name from a male lineage; she is told fairy tales in which men are the victors and women those who make sacrifices; she receives a male-centered education; she is taught to worship male gods; she lives in a society governed by men; she absorbs male-favoring views of power, knowledge, beauty, sexuality, and so on. As Shirley Chisholm, the first black and the first female US presidential candidate, said, "The emotional, sexual, and psychological stereotyping of females begins when the doctor says, 'It's a girl.'"

In writing as critically as he did, Fanon did not wish to victimize black men any further. Instead, as he said, "My true wish is to get my brother, black or white, to shake off the dust from that lamentable livery built up over centuries of incomprehension." In other words, only by exposing the fraud of white superiority did Fanon believe it could become ineffectual.

Women's survival depends on our realization that male superiority too is a Fraud, with a capital *F*. From the moment a boy is born, society socializes him into manhood, tells him to "man up," be a "little man," "act like a man," and all kinds of imperatives that discourage him from showing his sensitive and feminine side. Yet, in reality, from the moment a boy is born, he is entirely dependent on women to feed him, nurture him, cater to him, care for him, and comfort him. Girls, by contrast, are taught that to "act like a woman" is to be dependent, inferior, and weak, and yet the reality is that girls are the ones who have tools to feed, nurture, cater, care for, and comfort themselves.

The psychosocial story of womanhood and manhood is so misleading that even while women are generally more psychologically self-sufficient, they behave as if they weren't. Conversely, although men typically rely on women for care and nurturing, they act as if they don't. Women generally have to develop both their logical *and* emotional skills, whereas men are mainly encouraged to develop their logical skills. Yet as far as the psychosocial narrative goes, men are viewed as the more balanced gender. Men claim the position of being more intellectual than women and accuse women of being sensitive. Men simultaneously claim to be the greatest artists even while art is a field that requires great sensitivity.

Even when it comes to physical strength—that bastion of manhood—it is simply not true that physical strength validates male superiority. Throughout history, women have carried out a considerable portion of backbreaking work, from fetching heavy buckets of water to washing laundry by hand to cooking pots of food in often harsh conditions to tending to bruised men to birthing and raising children. These are all strenuous physical activities that women have carried out all while being told (and believing!) that they are physically weak. Women break through everything and go on living. If the consequences of the Fraud weren't so devastating, the deception and trickery would be laughable.

Returning then to the Europatriarchal Knowledge about womanhood. The Fraud cannot be exposed nor grasped only cerebrally, because the very idea that a person's intelligence quotient (IQ) is more important than their emotional quotient (EQ), and if I may add, their ethical-, empathy- or mindfulness quotient is part of the Fraud.

We need the evidence-based language that equips women

with the facts about male supremacy but we also need an evocative language that helps us grasp the Fraud inwardly, viscerally, and swiftly like a light bulb being switched on. "Reality requires a total understanding," Fanon wrote. "On the objective as on the subjective level a solution has to be supplied."

In the case of womanhood, such a language must, therefore, serve at least three purposes. First, it must end the delusion and deception of male superiority. Second, it must provide an opportunity to rethink the values of womanhood and to combat the rigidity in previous thinking about it. And third, it must itself convey a message of malleability and movement.

Fostering such a language is not an easy task, or feminists would not have been laboring at it for centuries. I think of the existentialist philosopher Simone de Beauvoir, who in her robust and original work, *The Second Sex*, insisted that womanhood is a social construct. Or the radical feminist author of *The Dialectic of Sex*, Shulamith Firestone, who staged a mock burial of "traditional womanhood." Or feminist philosopher Nina Power's scathing critique of contemporary feminism in her book *One-Dimensional Woman*, where she made the observation that the genius type "typically possesses feminine characteristics—imagination, intuition, emotion, madness—but is not, of course, an actual woman." They all explore new approaches to the language of womanhood, if within a Europatriarchal context.

Black and African feminists have also reshaped discussions of womanhood in what we might call Afropatriarchal societies. For example, the Nigerian feminist sociologist Oyeronke Oyewumi provided a new view that gender is not the primary way of signifying relationships of power in Africa. Instead, she argued in *African Women and Feminism* that factors such as seniority and kinship were equally if not more prominent symbols of power, and each individual occupied a "multiplicity of intersecting and overlapping positions, with varying relationships to privilege and disadvantage."

Others have challenged Oyewumi's arguments, such as Bibi Bakare-Yusuf, a publisher and intellectual whose views I agree with in this instance and who argues that while seniority and kinship indeed played crucial roles in Yoruba society, gender binary hierarchies also did manifest in Yorubaland, where Oyewumi based her research. In her study of Nnobi culture in eastern Nigeria, anthropologist Ifi Amadiume found that due to Igbo myths of origin, womanhood and manhood in precolonial Nnobi were flexible and not necessarily linked to biological sex, meaning that through varying practices and rituals Nnobi women could occupy positions usually assigned only to men and thereby exercise power and authority over both women and men. Amadiume also points to the Lunda and Swazi in southern Africa, the Bamileke in Cameroon, the Chamba in Nigeria, the Ashanti of Ghana, the Bemba of Zimbabwe, the Nupe in Nigeria, the Babamba and Mindossi in Congo, and the Mende of Sierra Leone as examples of societies where gender fluidity seems to have existed prior to colonization.

To put it simply, many feminists have engaged with the question of language and womanhood, and I place this book in that same tradition. However, while most have critiqued old meanings of femininity, it often involves instances of women successfully appropriating male socialization, such as in Nnobi society. Fewer have directly approached the topic of womanhood with a new conceptual outlook that centers women. There is a difference between a woman whose strength comes from emulating men and one whose strength emanates from her womanness. Those few that have approached the topic with women at the center include the Radicalesbians group, with their concept of the woman-identified woman, describing it as when "we see ourselves as prime, find our

centers inside of ourselves," or the French feminist Hélène Cix-
ous's notion of *écriture féminine,* the idea that women's writing
differs from men's literature as it gives voice to the body and the
emotions as well as the mind. These are such extraordinary and
essential hypotheses about womanhood that they leave you longing for more, and in my case also longing for a language of womanhood that is simultaneously Afropolitan—global *and* African.
What are the qualities of womanhood, or of the adult personhood
of a woman? If womanhood were not centered on manhood—if
manhood were merely complementary to womanhood in a mal-
leable way, as commas and colons punctuate a language—what
might the language of womanhood be?

Before considering these questions, it is first of all necessary
to note that both womanhood and manhood are constructs. The
need to redefine womanhood is not about further essentializing
the made-up constructs but about reconfiguring them so that instead of dimininshing women's lives individually and collectively,
they can enrich them. Although critiques of the sex-gender distinction often include questioning the viability of women as a
single group, I agree with the feminist philosopher Iris Young,
who argued in *Intersecting Voices*, "Without some sense in which
'woman' is the name of a social collective, there is nothing specific
to feminist politics." There are expressions that manifest uniquely
when the embodied experience is inflected by what we refer to as
womanhood. Yet I also believe (as Young also does) that any useful outlook on womanhood must be one that includes women of
all races, ethnicities, classes, sexualities, genders, and religions and
that indeed binds women through the narrative of womanhood
rather than through the biology of womanhood.

To speak of "women" as a category, first, is not by any means
to talk of a homogenous group, just as to mention big cats is not

to say that they all are jaguars, tigers, panthers, or lions. Second, the development of a comprehensive language of womanhood is an endless and ever-changing task. If the narrative I am initiating using the color blue has value, then it will create a gestalt in the reader's perception and will beget its own deepening. Third, as I have suggested thus far, any redefining of womanhood that will benefit women cannot itself follow the patriarchal mode of producing meaning. For this reason, my understanding of womanhood is shaped by the mind and the passions; the intellect and the emotions; the felt, the lived, and the observed. It is an understanding informed by years of engaging with the literature on the topic in both the sciences and the humanities, but it is equally an understanding that is deeply personal and thus best unified through creative expression, political conceptualization, and personal experience, by Sensuous Knowledge.

On that note, my sense is that womanhood in itself, when it is whole, self-contained, and not spinning around the axis of maleness, holds life in the way that the ocean holds breath. It is like water, in the way that water is soft and fluid but also lethal if it floods or engulfs you. It is like a womb in the way that a uterus is an enclosing where everything is created. Womanhood is like a wave; it rises with the tides, it swells with life, and it crashes against any obstacles in its way before calmly making its way to its destination.

Womanhood is embodied by the color blue not only because of the cultural meanings of blue but also because blue—and color generally—is an undervalued source of knowledge about human identity. Colors can offer explanations, or more precisely, they can lend their qualities and characteristics to a deepening understanding of ourselves. Blue is the color of wholeness and unity; it represents the confluence of the sky and the seas where the earth becomes one. Blue is a color that is delicate and bold at once. It reflects the peaceful blue of heaven and the intuitive blue of the night. Blue is the color of longing, melancholy, and sorrow. Blue is music. Blue is also the color that is associated with power. It is therefore the color that the patriarchal world links to maleness. Baby boys wear blue, and male politicians wear blue, men's grooming items are blue, the militaries wear blue. Yet as we now know, blue is a feminine color in Africa.

Waning Gibbous

I have a blue chiffon dress that I love. It is a special kind of blue—azure, shimmery, and light pastel, like the lustrous blue color of the sky. For years, my blue dress was rolled into a bundle at the bottom right corner of my wardrobe in Sweden. Then it moved along with me to Spain and to New York and to London and to Lagos, only to inhabit the same position—crumpled into the smallest possible mound of fabric, stashed into the corner of each wardrobe it occupied, unworn. It's the dress I wore the night that I was raped.

I'd noticed David as soon as he walked into the nightclub. He looked like an African god, and despite myself, I walked over to him and pulled him to the dance floor. We danced suggestively, spoke very little, and exchanged numbers.

We met again the following weekend. Immediately I sensed something different about him; he was less friendly, less flirtatious. He seemed detached and didn't ask many questions. I texted my friends to say that I might join them later after all.

Before finishing my second drink, I went upstairs to the bathroom. As I headed back down, I felt strangely dizzy and wondered how I could be so drunk after barely two drinks. Waddling my way down the bathroom stairs is the last I remember of the evening.

My next memory is lying on a mattress at twilight, my body denuded of its inviolability by a handful of preying, aggressive men. I tried to scream, but all that came out was a whisper. When the men finally stopped and left the room, I decided to stand, but I was so drugged that I immediately fell back on the mattress. I tried to regain control of my body for what seemed an agonizingly long time. When I eventually got up, I could not find my clothes. I covered my body with my hands and walked toward the living room, where I found the men watching football. I asked them where my clothes were, but they didn't seem to hear me. I walked toward another room and pushed the door open. There, in the right corner, was my blue dress, crumpled into a small ball, as it has been ever since.

After the attack, I began having rape nightmares. Often in the dreams, the perpetrator would be a man that I admired, trusted, or loved. Perhaps this was because the men who raped me were Africans, "brothers," the group of men that I always felt the most affinity with. Sometimes there was no actual sexual violence in the dreams, just the ghost of it, which was enough for me to awaken trembling. The dreams triggered a primal emotion in me—not only fear but terror. Not merely terror but fury. It was not merely fury either; it was a rage. I could not fall back asleep because I was so enraged.

The story of my blue dress is evocative, but I do not share it to evoke sorrow. I'm not sad about it anymore, if sad is what I ever indeed was. The emotions I most associate with the crime are terror, fury, and rage. These were the emotions that arose in my recurring dreams because they were the emotions that I needed to process in order to heal.

No two women have the exact same reaction to sexual violence, and I know there are readers for whom my account will have a triggering impact. You are not alone. Whatever your reaction was, it is one that you should not need to experience. That is why I'm sharing the story, especially in a context of the language of womanhood. We have such collective terror, fury, and rage, as well as sorrow and many other emotions, because of the destructions of men. Whether it is rape, domestic violence, molestation, sexual harassment, or "just" the casual sexism and the quotidian abuse of power that surrounds us or that affects people whom we love, we have all borne witness to the recklessly raw, cold, and violent side of masculinity.

We have all glimpsed, if not been forced to stare into, the ambivalent gaze of a man whose soul is empty, occupied only by disgust for himself and consequently for everyone else. The visceral effect of bearing witness to this nihilistic side of masculinity shapes womanhood more than we are allowed to express. When we do give voice to this deeply ancestral truth, we are treated as though we have trespassed against a social contract. Yet it is a fact as old as humanity itself that women are forced to live in a world where male antipathy poses a violent threat.

Here's why we are silent about rage: we are conditioned to protect men who are not violent by refusing to speak about those who are. Deep in the female psyche, we feel a need to protect innocent men, or we lose our purpose. At most, society allows us to talk of a "woman's intuition," which is just a sweet and unthreatening way of expressing the terror, fury, and rage at the state of things that a woman carries in her subconscious.

But if we protect those men who are not violent at the cost of our own well-being, who will protect us? How can we gain self-knowledge and share intimacy with others if we lie to ourselves? There is nothing wrong with protecting and caring for men who protect and care for women, but if we can't fully express the horror of living under the threat of male violence, then are we truly protected or is it an act? Very few men have ever been made to comprehend the extent of the female fear in patriarchy. Heck, very few women understand it themselves. We must reconfigure womanhood into a state where women can put themselves first.

This is not to say that womanhood is entirely devoid of violence and brutality. Deep down, we know that womanhood is not pink, sweet, and innocent. There is a blues, a darkness, a primal and feral autonomy to womanhood. Yet, as Audre Lorde writes in her essay "Poetry Is Not a Luxury," "For each of us as women, there is that dark place within where hidden and growing our true spirit rises."

Womanhood involves, for every woman if in different ways, a reckoning with patriarchy. It is the point when a woman ceases to cajole and coddle the male-dominating value system and decides not to accept the structures that seek to destroy her but instead to grow her character in those spaces where there has been injury and confrontation.

The reckoning can be triggered by myriad events—the witnessing or experiencing of a crime, the exclusion from power structures or the awareness raised by movements such as Me Too. What is sure is that the moment of reckoning is never easy. Some women go into denial while others become defensive or (self-)destructive; some take their revenge while others cling, weep, or despair.

In my case, after being raped, I began to cultivate a sense of disaffected stoicism. I blocked out the incident and bottled up the trauma, which eventually made me reckless, feeling so invincible that I put myself in further risky situations.

It took time, but my experience ultimately taught me that just as when the body suffers injury the wound must be tended, so when the spirit suffers injury its wounds also must be tended. Otherwise they appear to heal, only to return as a chronic psychological ache.

Whatever experiences cause the reckoning, it is important to honor the full range of emotion and to enable healing in the gentlest possible way. It means allowing the rage to surface but then committing to the business of living, loving, and filling our lives with meaningful joy, not despite male violence but because we have seen firsthand what the absence of love and joy in the human spirit looks like. It may sound like a cliché, but the absolute triumph over violation comes from making ample space in your life for love and preventing the paralysis of indifference from taking root.

If there is one thing that men are unquestionably superior at, it is violence. We should never ignore the fear that men's superiority at violence subjects women to, but neither should we allow that fear to become the thing that governs our lives, or we will never become self-governed. Conversely, if we never become autonomous, the injustices will never end.

For some reason when you put a woman in nature, she automatically wants to touch the trees, the lakes, the soil. She wants to be caressed by it too, and so she hugs nature's branches, streams, and fields.

If we are not mindful, especially given that women are socialized to appropriate the male psyche, women too will slip into the abyss of enmity and emptiness produced by Europatriarchal Knowledge. Humanity is ultimately reciprocal and interwoven, and what a man can do, a woman also can do, and vice versa.

It is in the space between injury and healing, between trauma and triumph, and between the accepting of what is while committing to what can be that an empowering language of female adulthood is built.

Full Moon

I began this chapter with a personal telling of the story of Goddess Asi of the Foya Kamara, which I originally read in a book about indigo fabric, as told by American craftswoman Esther Sietmann Warner Dendel.

To me, the color blue in the story represents womanhood, in the sense of female adulthood and personhood discussed throughout this chapter. The psychosocial inference in the story is that Asi yearns for the color blue because she yearns for womanhood. Yet in order to acquire womanhood, Asi must lose her girlish innocence, which is what her baby represents. The death of the baby is a drastic measure, but as the psychoanalyst and author Clarissa Pinkola Estés writes in her book "Women Who Run With the Wolves," a brutal episode in stories is "embedded with instructions which guide us about the complexities of life." The baby dies in the story so that we can grasp the importance of womanhood to Asi. And because innocence is a part of joy, the loss of innocence is a profoundly sorrowful experience. However, the spirits promise Asi that she will have a new baby if she shares the secret of the color blue only with women. The spirits in the story represent feminism, the movement that, as Young put it earlier, is nothing specific "without some sense in which 'woman' is the name of a social collective." The ultimatum the spirits give Asi is thus a symbolic message of sisterhood in the political sense that will be discussed in the next chapter. Ultimately, the instruction in the story of Goddess Asi is that all women must go through a reckoning with patriarchy to receive the gift of womanhood.

I'm reminded of Toni Morrison's commencement address to the all-female Wellesley College class of 2004. In it she said, "There is nothing . . . more satisfying, more gratifying than true adulthood. The adulthood that is the span of life before you. The process of becoming one is not inevitable. Its achievement is a difficult beauty, an intensely hard won glory, which commercial forces and cultural vapidity should not be permitted to deprive you of."

Also, a photo of Winnie Madikizela-Mandela comes to mind. It was taken in 1977, during Winnie's exile in Brandfort, by the photographer Peter Magubane, her friend. At this point, Winnie had spent the last thirteen years of her life intermittently imprisoned, banned, on trial, restricted, and detained. Yet the apartheid regime had not succeeded in quenching her resolve, and so they sent her into exile in Brandfort, an impoverished rural province where Winnie knew no one and couldn't speak the language but where she eventually not only set up a preschool and a clinic but also radicalized the previously depoliticized community.

In the photo she leans against a wire fence. She is wearing a T-shirt that says "Prisoner No. 2382981, Government Property, not to be removed from prison" across it. At first, it's challenging to decipher the expression on Winnie's face. As in so many photos of her, there's a mixture of moods—defiance, hurt, sorrow, irascibility, fearlessness, strength, vigilance. However, once the impressions of the image settle, what is left in the mind's eye is an image of a woman who is a woman not because of what it means to be a man, certainly not because of whom she married, but because she is independently and wholly woman. A WOMAN in capital letters like the color blue; tall like the sky, free, concerned, deep, and utterly liberated if concerned.

Yet the Europatriarchal narrative typically misconstrues Winnie's story. So that we'll condemn her, there is an emphasis on Winnie's later life—her love affairs, her involvement in the Mandela United Football Club, and in particular her radical political views that made reconciliation with Nelson impossible. Because, of course, her refusal to simply be "Mandela's wife" is punishable.

Winnie is regularly portrayed as the sweet love interest of Nelson Mandela, later taking on her husband's struggle, only to eventually turn into a bitter, dangerous woman. In truth, Winnie was never the innocent, sweet girl she is portrayed as when she met Nelson. She was already determined and independent. She was by then the first black medical social worker in South Africa. She was a young woman who ran away from her family to avoid traditional marriage. Also, she had turned down a US scholarship to remain active in the African National Congress. Neither did she simply fight her husband's struggle. She fought her battle, the black struggle and the women's struggle. And she did not turn into a bitter woman; she turned rather into a wronged woman. She became who she did in a society that treated her and her kin with cruelty. Yes, Winnie was "un-neat." She was a troublemaker, a political icon, a woman who made heavy sacrifices for the struggle, a symbol of resistance, a femme fatale, and a matriarch.

Winnie's last journal entry in solitary confinement is a request for the return of her confiscated properties. It includes, among other things, "1 blue dress." When I read this in her memoir, I couldn't help but think of her request for the return of that blue dress also as a request for the replacement for the very thing that her society—that our societies—be it the racists, the sexists, or the greedy capitalists—always sought to steal, womanhood.

It is not clear whether she received her items back, but like many women before and after her who dared not only to challenge, fight back, and resist but also to dive in, live, and love, she received back the one thing that matters: her womanhood, the autonomy of female adult personhood.

Once in a Blue Moon

Once in a blue moon, a total solar eclipse is visible from a different location on the earth's surface. A solar eclipse takes place when the earth, moon, and sun are aligned in what is known as a syzygy, which is when three or more celestial bodies configure in a straight line. When a solar eclipse occurs, on average every one and a half years, hundreds of thousands of people flock from near and far to witness the rare occasion. They later give testimonies about how in those brief seconds when the moon's perspective—rather than the sun's—illuminated the world, they too were changed by experiencing the world as a place of mystery, luminosity, and playfulness. They share that the solar eclipse brings with it a sense of unity and rejoicing.

In many cultures, the moon is symbolic of womanhood while the sun is symbolic of manhood. If we stick with that metaphor, the solar eclipse corresponds with the silencing of women that takes place in our societies and with the healing and joy that emerge when we end the silencing.

During a solar eclipse, the moon does not seek to annihilate the sun; it merely obscures it. By offering the color blue as a schema to guide a new set of attitudes and images about womanhood, it is not my intention to declare that blue cannot also be a masculine color or that men cannot or do not possess the qualities that I have attributed to womanhood. By contrast, from the myth of the goddess Asi of Liberia to women's ritualistic use of the blue gemstone lapis lazuli in ancient Egypt to the indigo blue Adire of Yorubaland to my blue dress and to Winnie's, what we see is that the color blue has a more complex history than Europatriarchal narratives suggest with their blue overalls for baby boys and blue suits for powerful men. These woman-centered narratives reveal how we are deeply conditioned into our identities as women and men but also how these are all just stories; we are also freer and less constrained to gender norms than is generally believed, regardless of how we identify.

of SISTERHOOD

There is a passage in Chimamanda Ngozi Adichie's novel *Half of a Yellow Sun* where, during the beginnings of the Biafra war, Kainene finds out that her twin sister, Olanna, had sex with her boyfriend, Richard. In their ensuing confrontation, Kainene ends the conversation with three words: "It was unforgivable."

The next time the sisters see each other, months have passed, and the war has advanced. Both sisters have witnessed war atrocities of an enormity they could never imagine. They embrace, and Kainene says, "There are some things that are so unforgivable that they make other things easily forgivable." Moments later, Kainene slips her hand into Olanna's.

It is a scene that perfectly captures the intricacies of sisterhood and female bonding, that multilayered fabric made of love, anger, betrayal, reconciliation, and tenderness that is framed by the awareness of a common enemy—in the novel, war; in the case of all women irrespective of their race, class, or sexuality, patriarchy.

Yet although patriarchy is an equal-opportunity oppressor that subjects all women to tyranny regardless of their class, race, nationality, religion, or sexual orientation, it polarizes women as a group. Women's racial, class, and sexual differences create divisions and wounds that calcify into resentment, guilt, and enmity.

In this polarized environment, where differences between women-of-color feminists and white feminists, between trans women and cis women, even between black diaspora and indigenous African feminists, and so forth, are emphasized, sisterhood seems unfashionable. But it is one of the most crucial concepts if women are to eliminate patriarchy in the twenty-first century.

The sisterhood I refer to is not the sentimental interpretation of the term but rather the feminist sense of political solidarity between women. It's what bell hooks referred to as "true Sisterhood" in her book *Ain't I a Woman: Black Women and Feminism*. True Sisterhood confronts racism, classism, and homophobia so women can stand in political solidarity against patriarchy. As bell hooks wrote in "Ain't I a Woman: Black Women in Feminism," even "the most uninformed and naive women's liberationist knows that Sisterhood as political bonding between women is necessary for feminist revolution."

In addition to political solidarity, I mean sisterhood as a notion that reflects love for women. Love for women is not the same as everybody getting along—we don't have to be friends with every feminist—but we need to love women, and women's specific history, knowledge, and traditions, to want an end to their oppression.

Feminism is a struggle *against* patriarchy, but it is equally a struggle *for* sisterhood. To be a feminist is to be an initiated woman, one awakened in opposition to the patriarchal oppression of women. Not just the oppression of women of one's own race, one's age, one's tribe, and one's class but of *all* women. Not only the specific type of patriarchal oppression that most affects one's life but *all* patriarchal oppression.

Audre Lorde famously said in "The Transformation of Silence into Language and Action," "It is not difference which immobilizes us, but silence. And there are so many silences to be broken." Lorde included a version of this quote in almost all the talks that she gave about feminist sisterhood, and you could argue ultimately that almost all Lorde's talks were about sisterhood. If there was one message that was central to her body of work, it was that of sisterhood—not as "pathological" but as "redemptive," not "advocating mere tolerance of difference" but that our "strength lies in recognizing difference as a source of power."

Our differences still immobilize us. There are still so many silences to be broken. We still have to fight "for that very visibility which also renders us most vulnerable, our Blackness," as Lorde continued in the essay.

Despite black women's essential contributions to the feminist movement, we receive the least "return on investment," if I may sound entrepreneurial. Gloria Steinem, the feminist icon whose primary message, like Lorde's, has always been to strengthen political sisterhood, said in an interview in "Black Enterprise," "Black women invented the feminist movement." It wasn't a hyperbolic statement. Feminism wouldn't exist if not for black women.

The first wave of feminism in the nineteenth century emerged out of the antislavery movement. Women such as Elizabeth Cady Stanton and Susan B. Anthony may have been the front figures of feminism then, but their advocacy was shaped by previously enslaved African women such as Anna J. Cooper and Ida B. Wells, who didn't have the racial privilege to be lead figures in the movement.

The second wave of feminism also arose from the Black Liberation. It became known as *Women's* Liberation precisely because it was influenced by *Black* Liberation, which in return drew inspiration from *Third* World Liberation movements.

The third wave of feminism was started once again by a black feminist, the writer Rebecca Walker, in an article for *Ms.* magazine. The fourth wave ultimately would hardly be what it is without movements like Me Too, also created by a black woman, Tarana Burke, as well as theories such as intersectionality, developed by black feminist thinker Kimberlé Crenshaw to describe the ways that racism and sexism impact women's lives in tandem. Famous black feminists such as Beyoncé and Chimamanda Ngozi Adichie are arguably the most iconic feminists of our time. Not only did black women invent the feminist movement, as Steinem put it, we also invigorate it.

If black feminists invented the movement, lesbian feminists have reinvented it time and again. The feminist movement owes much of its success to the radical perspectives brought to it by lesbians.

At the Second Congress to Unite Women in New York City in 1970, a group of lesbians who called themselves the Lavender Menace staged a flash mob against the self-defeating hypocrisy of discriminating against some women in a movement that claimed to champion sisterhood. They chose the name in response to a homophobic remark made by Betty Friedan, author of the classic feminist book *The Feminine Mystique*, who in the heyday of second-wave feminism complained that lesbians were a "lavender menace."

Homophobia was so rampant within the early contemporary feminist movement that when the Lavender Menace asked audience members to join them onstage, only a dozen women came forward. Later, the members of Lavender Menace formed a group called Radicalesbians, whose theories had a significant impact on politicizing feminism. Many of the critical feminist concepts we still engage with today, such as "woman-identified woman," "consciousness raising," and the "lesbian continuum," were first formulated by lesbian feminists such as Adrienne Rich, Rita Mae Brown, and Barbara Smith, members of Radicalesbians.

It should be noted that although only a dozen women came forward following the flash mob, by the next day, Lavender Menace workshops were filled. This points to a unique and essential characteristic of feminism, namely, that unlike most ideological movements, it takes criticism on board and improves.

Already at the first global feminist gathering, the International Congress on Women's Rights in Paris in 1878, the constitution of the organizing body, the International Congress of Women (ICW), claimed to be "a federation of women of all races, nations, creeds and classes." In theory. In practice, *international* meant "Western," *all races* referred to "white women," and *all classes* was in fact "privileged women." The congress merely reproduced global power structures within the feminist movement, structures that we are still battling with.

But following complaints about the structure of the ICW, by the end of World War I, the organization had added sections in Latin America, Asia, Africa, and the Middle East. By 1910, there was the first International Feminine Congress in Buenos Aires, which led to the UN World Conferences on Women in Mexico, Nairobi, and Beijing.

Likewise, when the second-wave writer and activist Robin Morgan popularized the notion of sisterhood in her 1970 anthology, *Sisterhood Is Powerful*, black women wrote only three of the anthology's fifty-seven articles. But after the whitewashing of the moment was criticized, the second and third volumes of Morgan's series, *Sisterhood Is Global* (1984) and *Sisterhood Is Forever* (2003), were inclusive and, therefore, more comprehensive feminist works. Also, these anthologies paved the way for other collected works about solidarity by women from all over the world, such as Cherríe Moraga and Gloria E. Anzaldúa's *This Bridge Called My Back: Writings by Radical Women of Color*; Nigerian feminist Obioma Nnaemeka's *Sisterhood, Feminisms & Power*; and Jennifer Browdy de Hernandez's *Women Writing Resistance: Essays on Latin America and the Caribbean*.

Keep in mind too that divisions within the feminist movement are not neatly segmented into race, sexuality, and class. Politics plays a big role as well: a white liberal feminist and a black liberal feminist may share more in common than a black radical feminist and a black liberal feminist. Conversely, a black radical feminist may find sorority with a white radical feminist more quickly than with a liberal black feminist.

The famous Combahee River Collective formed in part as a response to the heteronormative sentiment that its members, including Barbara Smith, Demita Frazier, and Audre Lorde, experienced in the National Black Feminist Organization (NBFO), which in 1973 formally cemented black feminism as a separate ideological movement. The Combahee River Collective met from 1974 to 1980, and its feminist statement continues to shape discussions on identity politics, intersectionality, and black radicalism today.

Perhaps the greatest division within the feminist movement is ultimately between women who are "breaking silences" and those who are "solidifying silences," as Lorde might say. As she put it in "The Transformation of Silence into Language and Action,"

"The women who sustained me . . . were Black and white, old and young, lesbian, bisexual, and heterosexual, and we all shared a war against the tyrannies of silence."

While writing this book, I participated in an event at Foyles, a landmark bookshop in London. During the Q and A, an audience member asked whether I thought that black feminists should collaborate with white feminists. I responded that we should, but conscientiously, without tolerating the abuse of power in any way. I added that just as we can't tackle white supremacy without our black brothers, we can't tackle patriarchy without all our sisters—white, brown, black, all women everywhere.

Afterward, a woman came to tell me that she disagreed and that we should not collaborate with white women. They don't care about the freedom of black women, she said. She did not speak to white women at all or white men, for that matter, unless she had to. To me, this seemed the ultimate victory of racism, to rancorously shape life around one's grievances. I thought of Toni Morrison's words at a commencement speech at Sarah Lawrence College:

> If I spend my life despising you because of your race, or class, or religion, I become your slave. If you spend yours hating me for similar reasons, it is because you are my slave. I own your energy, your fear, your intellect. I determine where you live, how you live, what your work is, your definition of excellence, and I set limits to your ability to love. I will have shaped your life. That is the gift of your hatred; you are mine.

However, later that night, as I reflected on our conversation, I wondered how much our circumstances affected our different positions. The person whom I love more than any other is a white woman, my mother. Thanks to this love, I feel intimately aware that white womanhood can represent safety, love, and friendship as well as a critical and conscientious approach to race and ethnicity, as my mother did, especially after living in Nigeria for almost four decades.

Also, I grew up in Nigeria and didn't experience racism from white people on a day-to-day basis until I moved to Sweden. Had I grown up in a different environment, such as 1980s Britain, as this woman did, where racial prejudice from white people was a daily factor, and where I had no direct, intimate relationship with whiteness, I too might have given up on interacting with white people; it might be too painful, risky, and tedious.

However, being a black woman with a white mother makes experiences of racism from white women all the more personally affecting. My memory is like a well of racially tinged incidents. There's the teacher who accused me of plagiarism when I wrote a story about a very personal experience in English class; the other teacher who always referred to me as a negress; the boss who told me that I was in Sweden and not Africa when I hadn't completed an assigned task; the girls who physically attacked me during my first month in my new school in Sweden while calling me *neger*, the Swedish version of the *N*-word; the publisher who rejected the proposal of this book because it was "too African." There's my grandmother, a woman whom I loved dearly, and who loved me even more, but who never seemed to see beauty and a cause for pride in me quite as easily as she did in my white cousins. There are shop assistants, dentists, interviewers, professors, airport staff, headmistresses, family members, friends, bank clerks, makeup artists, panel members, editors, journalists, and indeed white feminist colleagues all exerting racially charged power and privilege over me. Women of color and women from the Global South, which the vast majority of women in the world are, may face big and systemic obstacles because of the Europatriarchal machinery. But the day-to-day obstacles, the ones that ultimately affect the minutiae of life, are often presented to us by white women.

Also, I can't help but go back to Lorde, who grew up in an all-black family in 1940s Harlem, a place where race had a devastating impact on a black person's life. It both inspires and unnerves me that despite the harrowing racism that Lorde described in her memoir *Zami, a New Spelling of My Name: A Biomythography*, she made herself vulnerable to feminist sisterhood over and over again.

It shows how deeply committed she was to women's liberation. She didn't advocate for sisterhood because she'd gotten tired of addressing racism. Hardly—she wrote indefatigably about the effect racial prejudice had within the feminist movement. Lorde's life is a testament to her conviction that "where the words of women are crying to be heard," as she wrote in "The Transformation of Silence," "we must each recognize our responsibility to seek those words out, to read them and examine them in their pertinence to our lives. That we not hide behind the mockeries of separations that have been imposed upon us and which so often we accept as our own."

Notwithstanding, she gave so much while receiving little in return. She refused to "sit in our corners mute forever while our sisters and ourselves are wasted, while our children are distorted and destroyed, while our earth is poisoned." Yet, she wondered, in a letter to white feminist writer Mary Daly, how many white feminists truly "read my words, or did you merely finger through them for quotations which you thought might valuably support an already conceived idea . . . ?"

To boot, her feminist and LGBT advocacy alienated her from many in the black community. In response to an antifeminist article by Robert Staples, a black male sociologist, she wrote, "Freedom and future for Blacks does not mean absorbing the dominant white male disease of sexism. As Black women and men, we cannot hope to begin dialogue by denying the oppressive nature of male privilege."

It was this same message that informed my response during the Foyles Q and A. It is not enough for black women to struggle against racism if our goal is to live free and thriving lives. Whether it's psychological abuse, domestic and violent abuse, or girls being denied the same prospects as boys, crimes against black girls and women are mostly committed by black men. Even if we got rid of the racist system, we would still have to deal with the monster of patriarchy and destructive masculinity. It is a monster we cannot fight in hostile, fragmented groups.

A few days after the Foyles event, when walking home late at night on an empty street, the figure of another person appeared in the distance. I straightened my posture and walked firmly, as one does when there is a risk of confrontation, however small it might be. As the person drew nearer, I saw that it was a woman, and she was white. We smiled reassuringly at each other, as women sometimes do in places of potential danger. I continued walking when another person emerged, this time a black man. We walked past each other, and then I turned onto another empty street and continued listening to the podcast playing on my headphones.

Some minutes later, I felt a tap on my shoulder. Startled, I saw that it was the same man I'd walked past minutes earlier. He had followed me "just to say hi." Incensed that a man would think it okay to follow a woman, especially in the middle of the night on an empty street, I preemptively asked him if he was familiar with the story of witches with *vagina dentatas* (teeth in their vaginas that castrate rapists). It is not a strategy I necessarily recommend, but in my frightened state I gambled that he might, as an African man, recoil at the mention of witches and toothy vaginas. It worked, and he rushed off.

Still preoccupied with the Foyles event, and with this chapter, I saw that the incident illuminated how the patriarchal threat and the threat of white womanhood work in different ways. There is the institutionalized everyday racism I experience from white women, and there is the threatening sexism from men, black men included, also institutionalized.

Resistance against racism and sexism is like bench-pressing weights. If you lift only with your right hand, the left weight will collapse on you and vice versa. We need to resist sexism together with those black men who oppose it, and racism with white women who oppose it.

Without a sense of political sisterhood, the fight against patriarchy is moot. Acid rain may not kill every single tree in the world, but it is a threat to every single tree on this planet. Patriarchy is similarly a threat to every single woman in the forest of humankind. Ms. Hill quotes Jesus in the book of John, "I am the vine, and ye are the branches." Sisterhood is the vine, and our thorny and entangled connections are the branches of the vine.

We opened this chapter with the story of the sisters Kainene and Olanna and their scene of meeting again in *Half of a Yellow Sun*. Three key elements present in that scene are central to sisterhood within the feminist movement. These are forgiveness, responsibility, and conscientiousness.

Forgiveness is not something we do merely out of the goodness of our hearts; it is what we do when something more important than anger fills the heart. It is when we don't give others what Toni Morrison called "the gift of hatred." Forgiveness is never about forgetting the past; it is instead about placing more importance on well-being in the future.

Responsibility is what comes when we let go of guilt. If there is one thing that prevents otherwise mutual conversations between women of color and white women, it is guilt. All too often in feminist discourse, white women engage in self-flagellating and ultimately self-serving excursions of guilt. There may be a time and space to express a guilty conscience, but it is a useless emotion in fighting patriarchy if it does not lead to responsibility.

When *Half of a Yellow Sun's* Olanna merely felt guilty toward her sister, Kainene, her guilt prevented her from joining forces with her to alleviate the effects of war. When she took responsibility for her actions, acknowledged her wrongs, and committed to becoming a better companion, the sisters were able to build a relationship still with flaws and complexity but also with possibilities for solidarity.

Conscientiousness is the glue of sisterhood and solidarity. When we are conscientious, we live with careful and critical attention to our conscious choices. As feminists who oppose patriarchy and as women who must live within it, we practice conscientious feminism when our feminism does not give assistance to patriarchy but instead refuses to let it use divide and conquer to derail our goal of ending it.

Forgiveness, responsibility, and conscientiousness help foster a strong force of political sisterhood. None of them by itself removes all the obstacles to solidarity within the feminist movement, but together they can make those obstacles more surmountable.

There is an African story called "One Body," which I came across on a beautiful blog, *Wisdom Stories to Live By*, that illustrates these points. Allow me to retell it in closing:

The Body

Once upon a time various parts of the body began complaining that they didn't like the stomach. The hand said, "I cultivate all the soil to plant the seeds, I harvest the crops, I prepare the food. All that the stomach ever does is wait to be fed. How unfair." The feet agreed and said, "Yeah, me too, man. I carry the heavy stomach around all day, I carry her to the farm to get food, I carry her to the river to get water, I even carry her up the palm tree to get palm wine, and all the stomach ever does is lie there and expect to get her ration of food, water, and wine whenever she needs them. This is unfair." The head chimed in, complaining about how she carries all the heavy load from the farm and the river, having to do all the thinking—all to feed the stomach, who does nothing to help.

The parts of the body decided to embark on a protest action. They agreed to stop working and feeding the lazy stomach until the stomach ended her selfishness. A whole day went by, and they didn't give the stomach food or water or wine. All that the stomach did was groan from time to time while the others taunted her. By the second day of starving the stomach, however, the head said that she was beginning to feel dizzy. By the third day, the hands reported that they were feeling weak, and the feet were wobbly and could not stand straight. Then it dawned on them that, much as they were visibly supporting the stomach, the stomach was also helping them in a less obvious but equally important way. By feeding the stomach, they were feeding themselves without knowing it. So they called off their strike and went back to work to feed the stomach. Their strength returned, and together with the stomach, they continued to live.

Feminist sisterhood, you could say, is the belly of the collective body of women. It is a big challenge for feminism today, as it always has been, to understand that we are "one" body. It is not about the hand forcefully becoming a foot or the foot a hand. It is about cooperating and appreciating the hand and foot for what they are so that the body can function in the most healthy ways possible.

of POWER

One day they're going to open up my head and find a map of West Africa inside.

—Teju Cole

The future of our earth may depend upon the ability of all women to identify and develop new definitions of power.

—Audre Lorde

And they say to him, by what exousia [power] do you do these things?
And who gave you this exousia [power] to do these things?

—Mark 11:28

I.

Along the banks of the River Niger lives a fishing community known as the "masters of the river." They are the Bozo, founders of the famous city Djenné, which in pictures is reminiscent of ancient Egyptian towns with their mud-brick homes and courtyards. The resemblance is no coincidence. Many of West Africa's peoples, like the Bozo, migrated to the region from ancient Egypt five millennia ago, and their lifestyle remains so similar to the Nile

River people of the early Egyptian dynasties that should Pharaoh Hatshepsut herself visit these regions of Mali today, she would feel right at home.

The Bozo live in symbiosis with the River Niger. They wake to its lapping waves; they bathe in the river; they fish in it, play in it, and build their homes and temples of worship all in harmony with it. However, what the Bozo might not deduce from the River Niger, as I shall in this chapter, is an understanding of power. For if there is one concept that women must reevaluate and repurpose, it is power, and the history and character of the River Niger helps us to think about power differently.

As it stands, women are cut off from power altogether. The only time power is seen from a woman-centered point of view is when women use sex or the potential outcome of sex—procreation—to control and manipulate men. But even these pockets of power are enacted in domains that are male dominated—the family institution, the state, and so on. All other understandings of power, whether in terms of leadership, religion, academic rank, the law, or mental agility, are suffused with a male bias.

Even feminist analyses of power wade through the swamps of patriarchy trying to find their roots, when everyone knows that the more of a swamp's mud you accumulate, the deeper into it you sink. Take for example the slim yet stimulating book *Women & Power: A Manifesto* by classical historian Mary Beard. The book argues that women's powerlessness in modern society is tied to their lack of power in the myths and traditions of the classical world. In one of the earliest Greek dramas of 458 BCE, Clytemnestra becomes the effective ruler of her city while her husband fights the Trojan War, and subsequently she "ceases to be a woman," for a woman cannot rule. Two and a half millennia later, as Beard argues, the template for a powerful woman—as so many Western female political leaders, from Margaret Thatcher to Angela Merkel to Hillary Clinton show—is still a powerful man. It is a critical and captivatingly written argument. Yet Beard's book does little to challenge our views of power itself, for it defines power in the same patriarchal way that it always has been defined, as tied to the state and its institutions—the government, the military, parliament, local constituencies, and so on—all of which are all male dominated.

Beard herself admits that her analysis is part of the old thinking of power, which, as she says, is connected to "the upper echelons of national politics." Although her book doesn't attempt to redefine power, she stresses that "if women are not perceived to be fully within the structures of power, surely it is power that we need to redefine rather than women."

One of the relatively few books that do redefine power from a woman-centered value system is *Women Who Run with the Wolves,* written by Jungian psychoanalyst and storyteller Clarissa Pinkola Estés. Hers is not an explicitly feminist book, and neither is it directly a book about power. Yet by intertwining psychoanalytical research, criticism, and archetypical stories, Pinkola Estés unearths an untamed, wise, and sensuous collective feminine knowledge that imbues women with a sense of power that is otherwise unavailable to them because patriarchy devalues women's multi-layered ways of knowing. It is no wonder the book has become a cult classic for power-starved women around the world.

When I first read *Women Who Run with the Wolves* (indeed as a power-starved young woman in her twenties), it had the effect of removing a blindfold from my eyes. I'd recently moved to London from New York; I had a glamorous job; I'd had a number of meaningful relationships (and a number of meaningless ones too); I lived a socially active life in a quirky studio in London's trendy Dalston; I was a samba dancer doing shows with a troupe of fun women.

In my free time, I wrote and read poetry at open mic nights. It is a time that stands out as one in which I became truly independent, and I felt a corresponding sense of excitement about life. Yet the woman-centered value system in *Women Who Run with the Wolves* affected my world profoundly. It opened my eyes to how things that made me feel powerful were defined through a male prism. For example, I felt independent not because I understood independence on its own terms but rather because I could do anything a man could do. I could apply my masculine side to my work, my thinking, and my lifestyle. My life lacked a woman compass.

Neither was I as empowered in my relationships as I thought I was. Around that time, I had a lover with whom I felt safe. He was "profeminist," caring, kind. Then one day, I came home and found him watching porn on his computer, which I had no problem with per se, only this was the worst type imaginable. A woman was being penetrated with a dildo so large that her anus had expanded to the size of a large aubergine. She was screaming like a newborn as the object pumped in and out of her aggressively. The male actor drilled the dildo in and out of her butt saying, "Take it!" in crescendo with her bleating. I'd never seen anything like it before. These were the early days of shock porn—women being violently raped, choked, gagged, slapped, and so forth—which is now commonplace. It was clear that my lover wasn't turned on by it; apparently a friend sent him the link precisely because it was then a novelty. Plus, even if it had subconsciously aroused him, I wouldn't necessarily have been upset about it as long as we were attuned in bed and he did not try to introduce (to me) an off-putting sexist pornographic gaze into our lovemaking.

What bothered me was that the clip didn't bother him. Only someone who doesn't have to live with an omnipresent threat of male aggression could watch a woman being violated with the same neutral attitude with which they might watch cat videos. Under the influence of Pinkola Estés, I felt weak and hurt at the extent to which men rely on the subjugation of women to be entertained. I felt powerless.

More and more, I became beset with power—what it is, how it is gendered, what it means in our lives, and how we approach it. I observed how throughout history, men have conceptualized power to work in their favor. The typical patriarchal understanding of power has three common characteristics. First, power is tied to the state and its institutions—the government, military, parliament, local constituencies, and so on, which are all male dominated. Second, Europatriarchal Knowledge defines power in ways that are synonymous with terms such as *dominance*, *authority*, *violence*, *oppression*, and *coercion*, words that may be related to power but are not precisely the same thing. These definitions are then solidified through sociocultural practices that reinforce patriarchal meanings of power. Cultural depictions of power, whether in film, photography, literature, or paintings, feature typical representations of heroic, Machiavellian, patriarchal men such as James Bond or the Black Panther, or old photographs of African kings with their multiple wives and slaves surrounding them, or panegyrics to Mafia bosses in rap songs, or Casanovas surrounded by objectified women in advertisements, or navel-gazing tech bros in Silicon Valley. The list is endless.

The equation of power with dominance and coercion becomes obvious in academic writing. The political scientist Robert A. Dahl's formula of power is perhaps the most widely taught definition of the notion: "A has power over B to the extent that he can get B to do something that B would not otherwise do." This definition comes at the expense of other understandings of power—where, for instance, A affects B in a manner in *accordance* with B's interests, or A affects *A* in their *own* interests, or A's and B's decisions positively affect *the rest* of the alphabet, or, most thankfully, where we stop speaking about power in terms of A and B at all!

Not only did Dahl equate power with dominance, but he also defined it formulaically. Which brings me to the third patriarchal definition of power—power as a measurable concept: "If A . . . then B." Power is something that can be traded like currency. This is what another major voice in the definition of power, Talcott Parsons, who argues in *Power: Critical Concepts,* edited by John Scott, that power is the "generalized capacity to secure the performance of binding obligations by units in a system of collective organization when the obligations are legitimized with reference to their bearing on collective goals and where in case of a recalcitrance there is a presumption of enforcement by negative situational sanctions—whatever the actual agency of that enforcement."

The abstract writing hardly makes it clear, but what Parsons was arguing is that power circulates and is analogous to money because it is a medium of exchange. In other words, Parsons too was quantifying power. It is an undertaking that may be suited to academic purposes, but for those of us who have to fight for the power to govern our own lives, it is a one-size-fits-all measurement that is incompatible with real-life struggles.

Dahl and Parsons are far from the only thinkers who have turned power into a measurable entity. The psychologists John R. P. French and Bertram Raven categorized power into five distinct "points of power": coercive power, reward power, legitimate power, expert power, and referent power. Political theorist Steven Lukes sees three dimensions of power, which he classifies as decision-making power, agenda-setting power, and ideological power. Inasmuch as white men dominate the theorizing about power, it is no surprise that the same three characteristics can be traced at least to renaissance philosopher Niccolò Machiavelli's treatise on the topic, *The Prince*.

With the exception of philosophers such as Hannah Arendt and Mary Parker Follett, few women and hardly any people of color have had a significant influence on mainstream conceptualizations of power, although power has of course been a critical topic in progressive movements. When we do come across a female thinker in the mainstream canon, such as Arendt, whose theoretical approach to power is not exclusively tied to the state, is not conceptualized as dominance or coercion, and is not measurable per se, she is predictably accused of being out of line with the central meanings of power, as Lukes claims that Arendt is in *Power: A Radical View*. As Arendt wrote in *On Violence*, "Power springs up whenever people get together and act in concert," and violence "ends in power's disappearance." To speak of nonviolent power is therefore redundant, as power is always nonviolent. Follett defined power in a pragmatic feminist way as being "power with," which is based on solidarity and collaboration and enables the multiplication of individual talents and knowledge, rather than "power over," which seeks to undermine others.

In my view, power is not A nor B, "power to," "power over," or even necessarily "power with." Necessary as "power with" is, it would be more accurately described as collaboration or solidarity. I prefer to say, quite simply, "power is." I would like to explore power, therefore, as a phenomenon rather than a system, to understand it by observing it rather than by measuring it. This way, I will later also be able to observe if power has patterns.

As a phenomenon, power is a kind of force, reminiscent of what the Yoruba refer to as *ashe*, the Hindu as *prana*, and Japanese Shinto worshippers as *kami*. *Ashe* is a philosophical concept that describes a quality that is immanent in everything (humans, nature, songs, food) and without which there would be entropy. *Prana*, as guru Swami Satyananda Saraswati said, is not merely "the breath, air, or oxygen," as modern yogis may have heard. "Precisely and scientifically speaking," Saraswati wrote in *Yoga* magazine, "prana means the original life force." The Shinto concept of *kami* refers to the complex energy system and the sacred essence within natural elements, deities, humans, places, and even objects. Insofar as power is a phenomenon and an observable force, it has qualities of intentionality that are connoted by *ashe*, *prana*, and *kami*.

Power itself is neither female nor male, but women and men relate to power differently. The gendered language with which we speak about power is symptomatic of—and antecedent to—the gendered inequality in our structure of power. To change this structure, the narrative of power must itself be boldly reimagined. As the current structure of power is based on Europatriarchal Knowledge, the reimagining of power should be based on knowledge that includes all life; that which is immeasurable, embodied, sentient, fertile, indigenous, non-Eurocentric, decolonial, and feminist—Sensuous Knowledge. Also, for any redefining of power to have value in the twenty-first century, it must be concerned with how power is entangled with nature. Nature is a source of existential meaning or "a domain of analysis," as feminist philosopher Sandra Harding argues in her excellent essay "Women's Standpoints on Nature."

If one must measure power at all, the barometer would be what I call *exousiance*, a term I am coining from the ancient Greek word *exousia*, which means "power." To describe exousiance, think of dendritic patterns, which are the vast and continuing patterns that can be found in the bodies of all humans, animals, and everywhere in nature, and which are characterized by what I'll refer to as *branching*. Consider, for example, how a branch of a river breaks off from the main body of water and then into smaller branches, which further break off into even smaller branches. Or think of the branches of a tree, the veins in a leaf, the capillaries in living tissue, the air passages in the lungs, coral reefs, neurons, or lightning—all share the same dendritic pattern. Each of these fractal-like phenomena can be characterized by their branching quality, which is part of connectedness and reciprocity, as well as by their autonomy and self-realization.

You could say that power has the same branching system. It has a center of concentration from where it erupts, but as it branches out, it expands and multiplies, stretching outward in self-mirroring patterns as many times as possible until the branch ends become so thin that the process ceases, only to begin in another dendritic pattern within the ecosystem. Even when one particular cluster appears to end, its roots and function provide another cluster with the capacity to repeat the same process. Yet each group pushes toward its own completion as it meets obstacles in the way of the process. There is a tremendous amount of autonomous *and* reciprocal life force in each branching.

This entire process illustrates exousiance. The better that obstacles are overcome, the more exousiance an organism—individual or collective—can be said to have. And, like the chicken-and-egg question—which came first?—it is impossible to know if the source branch is the one that pushes forth power or if it is the second or third or fourth branch that births itself. All we can see is that this branching process is surrounded by urge and determination, by a passionate longing to manifest and be thrust into existence. That is power in pure form. With this imagery, we witness power as it is ("power is")—the individual and the collective enmeshed and separate, existing together and individually, in constant movement.

Were you to apply exousiance to a scenario where you felt powerless—for example, a boss expecting too much of you, a racist coming up with excuses not to provide you a service, or a lover being unreliable—when you employ exousiance, instead of feeling depleted, you understand events within the many branches of your journey, and how they all converge toward a goal. One part of your life is not working but others might be. You are able to observe yourself as a holistic organism within an interconnected ecosystem and resolve to move forward. Similarly, when it comes to groups of people, exousiance recognizes the external will of the group as well as the interior of it, which results in powerful focus rather than a powerless lack of clarity.

The independent process of exousiance is depicted perfectly in the surrealist paintings of nature by the Nigerian artist Abayomi Barber—works that at first glance seem strictly mystical because they convey dendritic branches of trees shape-shifting into human silhouettes or animal contours and shadows of nudes that are fecund with mystery. But the more one studies Barber's work, the more the appreciation of fractals so typical to African culture suggests "power is"—a wild yet focused phenomenon—as it winds its way under, above, around, or through our perceived reality assuredly, like gravity.

II.

A river is never still.

When it meets an obstruction, it moves under, above, around, or through whatever prevents it from flowing. When blocked, a river revolts with all its weight, including that of the streams and tributaries that pour into it, until it flows smoothly again. Rivers flow down mountains, valleys, and plateaus. They flow into lakes, ponds, and seas. With the help of gravity, they swirl, surge, and push toward their final destination, the ocean.

Power is to human beings what gravity is to rivers. It is the vital force that helps us flow through the meandering streams of life. It is what gets us out of bed in the morning. It is equally the tool with which we build movements, effect change, and counter oppression. Power is the kernel of human achievement.

Just as the river aims toward the ocean, so too do humans strive toward our ultimate goal: self-actualization. You might prefer to call the destiny where the streams of our desires converge by a different name—contentment, enlightenment, purpose, fulfillment, equipoise, no fucks given, whatever you like. But I favor psychologist Abraham Maslow's way of putting it in his famous essay about the pyramid of human needs, "A Theory of Human Motivation": "A musician must make music, an artist must paint, a poet must write, if he is to be ultimately at peace with himself. What a man can be, he must be. This need we may call *self-actualization*" (emphasis mine).

Rivers, like humans, face significant obstacles as they aim toward their respective goals. A river's flow toward the ocean is obstructed by human-created barricades—levees, weirs, dams, deforestation, loss of forest cover, and pollution. The human journey toward self-actualization too is full of obstacles. They may be psychological blocks—a person might, for example, experience difficulty achieving their desires due to a lack of support from their family. They might have low self-esteem or suffer from depression or bad luck. Everyone—female or male, black or white, of whatever background—faces some degree of psychological obstacles in the path to self-actualization.

However, barricades can also be socially constructed. Depending on your gender, ethnicity, sexuality, class, or race, they can follow similar patterns, such as when laws prevent a young woman from getting an abortion and she therefore misses an opportunity to pursue her desired life path, or when a same-sex couple is unable to marry legally, or when people are prevented from expressing their views because of state censorship, or when countries are denied their sovereignty due to imperialist aims, or when heterosexual women put their own needs to the side and prioritize their partners' self-actualization. These are examples of "institutionalized oppression," to use the corresponding academic term, meaning that they are obstacles that are systematic and re-inforced by established laws, customs, and practices. Humans and rivers share one of the greatest institutionalized oppressions of our times, global warming, whose worst culprits are Europatriarchal corporation-nations and whose most affected victims are nature, women, and the impoverished people in the Global South, who suffer more illness, famine, and poverty because of climate change than any other population in the world. Rivers reflect the things that we associate with power; history, economics, and modernity all have been shaped amid the paths of the world's great rivers. Rivers have also shaped myths about gender. Many societies have tended to associate rivers with the feminine, so there is Lorelei of the River Rhine, Yemoja of the Ogun River, and Isis of the Nile.

Here I am not interested in reviewing myths and beliefs already told but rather in exploring nature, in the spirit of Sandra Harding's argument mentioned earlier, as a "domain of analysis." Can dialogue with nature (in this instance, rivers) with focused intent reveal patterns that demonstrate the essential quality of something, in this case, power? As Harding goes on to say, "From the beginning, feminist standpoint analysts took as their domain not only social worlds but also nature and the natural sciences. In addition to women's 'bodily knowledge' and women's different understandings of environmental processes, there was the obvious fact that it was mainly (but not exclusively) women historians, biologists, philosophers, and researchers and scholars in other disciplines who were producing the less sexist and androcentric readings of nature. . . ." What does a river itself, without our mythical conceptualizations, teach us about power? If rivers could speak about power, what would they, first of all tell us?

They would teach us to revolt. By *revolt*, I do not necessarily mean act through violence but rather to rise up, rebel, resist, and refuse to have your power taken from you by all means necessary. They would echo Ms. Hill, who says the only way to get out of oppression is through confrontation rather than through "retreat" or "running away." They would show that to become empowered as a river, to flow through obstructions—as the river does—requires that we identify and revolt against (or confront) the obstacles that prevent exousiance, the flow of power. If the accurate obstructions are not identified, the movement does not run smoothly; it dashes against the barrier, risking exhaustion. There is real power in clearly perceiving the obstacles in the way of self-actualization.

Rivers also teach us that not all revolts are the same. When some rivers revolt, the consequences are catastrophic. Such was the case, for instance, when in 1931 the world's third-largest river, the Yangtze, which has underpinned Chinese civilization for centuries, took hundreds of thousands of lives in one of the deadliest floods in human history. In the postdiluvian years, authorities expeditiously built dams along the Yangtze to prevent future catastrophes. And yet, as she surges from her source on the Tibetan Plateau to her mouth at the port of Shanghai, year after year, due to violent floods, countless people take their last breaths amid the deluge of the Yangtze.

Not all rivers are as vengeful as the Yangtze. The River Thames, to take another example, is comparatively polite, as per British custom. Despite human-created barriers that disrupt her flow, the Thames moves along with the status quo, adapting to the forever changing cities that she passes through. She throws her fair share of tantrums, of course. In 1928 the river swelled over into the heart of central London, killing a dozen people and making thousands homeless. Neither is it guaranteed that the Thames will not overflow in the future. In fact, potential flooding of the river is one of the greatest, yet barely talked about, threats to safety in twenty-first-century London.

The River Niger, to return to our West African muse, is not as belligerent as the Yangtze or as jejune as the Thames. Instead, she is calm and unaffected at first glance; she follows her course rather predictably, meaning she does not tend to erupt in violently deadly floods. However, as she journeys through the terra-cotta-colored Sahelian lands toward the Atlantic Ocean, those who disrupt her flow do so at a costly price.

The Suffragettes, Mau Mau rebels, Black Panthers, and the anarcho-syndicalist militias of the Spanish Civil War—and more recently protesters in London, Cairo, Paris, Hong Kong, Bolivia, Chile, Iran, and Baltimore—are examples of groups who, like the Yangtze, felt they had no choice but to resort to violent revolt in order to reclaim their power.

By contrast, you could compare the Thames to women, who have been toiling, carrying burdens, and performing labor for centuries, only to have scraps thrown at us in return. All in all, the women's struggle has been timid but for unexpected eruptions, such as the fight for women's suffrage, the invention of the birth control pill, women's armed revolutions in Africa during the continent's independence struggles, and the eruption of the Me Too movement. These events are a reminder that just as the Thames may flood at any minute, so too may a woman somewhere raise her voice, and her words may ripple and ripple until they cause a flood of change.

But no river tells a more captivating story about how to revolt against institutionalized oppression than the mostly unsung and mysterious River Niger.

In 1788 the African Association was founded, a British club with the intention to "set off on expeditions to discover the source, course and mouth of the River Niger." Led by Sir Joseph Banks, the association at first focused on the "exploration" of West Africa, but the more explorers it commissioned and the more information they gathered about West Africa's wealth, the more you could say its focus became the "exploitation" of West Africa.

One of the first, and undoubtedly the most famous, of explorers whom the association commissioned for its mission was the Scottish doctor Mungo Park, who learned that "travels in the interior districts of Africa," as the book he wrote upon his return—to great acclaim—was titled, were easier said than done. In fact, Park was one of the few men who made it back to England to tell the story. The first time, that is. When Park returned to the Niger nine years after his first mission, he joined the long list of men whose quest to conquer the river would be their last one.

Park was a profoundly racist man, yet his story complicates the idea that there can be nothing agreeable about such a character. As attractive as he was articulate, Park formed many friendships along his route. Aristocratic African women and royal concubines especially took to him for his good looks, and he took to them as well for theirs. Park's book and journals share accounts of beautiful African queens whom he encountered and whose "glossy jet of their skins, and the lovely depression of their noses" he praised.

In a posthumous monument honoring Park in Selkirk, where he was born, he is surrounded by a handful of women in an African town. He is lying on the ground fatigued and fevered after violent encounters with local warriors. The women wear sincere expressions of concern as they tend to him lovingly and adoringly.

The women's plaintive doting over Park is probably exaggerated, but there is a grace to their depictions rarely afforded African women in historical portrayals in Europatriarchal art, and that very aberration suggests to me that there might be a modicum of truth to the reciprocal relationship he had with African women.

But whatever mutuality there was in Park's attitude toward Africans during his first trip, it was gone when he returned nine years later, this time with the backing of the British state and an army of men. In contrast to his curious attitude during the first trip, this time he brought with him an utterly imperious and conquering spirit and a disregard of the people of the Niger and of the river herself. Within just a few months, Park and the majority of his men were dead.

In my school growing up in Nigeria, we were taught that, despite the unheroic destiny Park eventually met along the Niger, he discovered the great watercourse. In fact, although Park made it to the river's banks in Bussau (modern-day Niger State in central Nigeria), he never completed the mission that he was sent for—to discover its source and mouth. Try as they could, the British would require forty-three years and hundreds of men before a boastful, self-important man named Richard Lander, also a Scot, who also took to women of the continent—he even married an African woman offered to him by the Emir of Zaria in northern Nigeria today—satiated the curiosity of the African Association (by then called, as it remains, the Royal Geographical Society) by identifying the source and mouth of the mysterious African river.

This is not to say that Park or Lander "discovered" anything, even if they swam the length of the river from source to mouth. The Bozo, among many other people, lived in harmony with Joliba and Quorra, as the locals called the Niger long before Park was born. Stone Age tools dated more than thirty-nine thousand years old have been found along the Niger.

What the story we were taught in my school in Lagos misses is African agency. It perpetuates the fiction that Africans were passive to imperialism. In fact, Africans resisted; it is rare to come across a historical account of capitulation without a battle. The Nupe, the Igbo, and the kingdom of Benin all fought back against colonialism along the waterways of the Niger. Richard Lander and his entourage, to give one example of many, were attacked and detained by chiefs and rebels along the way—in Adamugu, Asaba, Aboh, and Akassa, just a few of the places that Landers's journal details. Ancient African kings fought back against dominance in every possible way—with their armies, with the extensive legal systems that existed in Africa at the time, through negotiations and treaties, and by playing the same game of divide and conquer, pitting the French against the English, for example—as they battled to defeat the Niger River. They rarely stood a chance, however. Not only did they not have the advanced weapons the enemy did, but also the geopolitical structure of Africa at the time consisted mainly of city-states, which were in trade competition with each other, if under amicable terms. When Europeans began their race to conquer Africa, they benefited from this structure, as the city-states were not poised to make a concerted effort since they relied on relatively healthy competition.

It is important to say, however, that it is *also* rare to find a historical account of agency without a corresponding report of greed. The truth is that the kings of the continent's empires, to stick with the example of kings, did what male leaders of empires have always done: they gambled with the fate of their people to win their own accumulation of power. Even those who defended their empires against European invasion were often rapacious and cruel men who treated slaves and women condescendingly. I'm thinking, for example, of Samory Touré, a self-taught scholar who became one of the Mali empire's most prolific leaders in the late nineteenth century. The French repeatedly tried to defeat Touré but failed, leading the French politician Gustave Humbert to say that he "fight[s] like Europeans, with less discipline perhaps but with much more determination as Douglas Porch accounts in "Wars of Empire." Touré was an anticolonial hero, but he built much of his empire by raiding the forests for slaves, whom he would later exchange of ammunition. As for women, Touré killed his own daughters for flirting with a palace page.

If anything worked against the smooth conquering of the River Niger, it was the River Niger herself. The river proved enigmatically uncooperative because, unlike most rivers, which move toward the ocean in the most straightforward possible way, the Niger takes a mind-boggling and capricious detour to reach her destination. Instead of flowing directly from the deep ravine in the Futa Jallon Highlands in Guinea, her source, to the swampy delta of Nigeria, her mouth, the Niger ventures north from Guinea through Mali, Niger, and Benin before looping her way south through Nigeria, where the limbs of her stream eventually branch out into the ocean.

Perhaps British explorers would have met a different fate if, rather than impetuously trying to conquer the River Niger, they had had the forbearance to cooperate with her and with the people who had already coexisted with the river for millennia. Instead, they mistook her calmness for docility. They tried to silence and manipulate her, but the Niger always had the last word. If Joseph Conrad's *Heart of Darkness* told the colonialist's story of Africa, the Niger tells Africa's account of the colonizer.

The Niger's wayward route is a fitting metaphor for power and the fate-like force of exousiance. First, consider the branching quality discussed earlier. Rivers start out as tiny streams at mountaintops. As the streams trickle down, they are met by other small streams and tributaries, together growing larger and larger until their mutual flow becomes a river. The more the river widens, the more power it has to circumvent the barriers in its way. In this sense, rivers show us that there is high power in collective action. Yet once a river reaches the ocean, its streams separate again, reminding us that in the end, each individual has their own journey to selfhood.

Second, the river reminds us that power is not necessarily tied to the state. States have derived a source of power from the world's rivers, but rivers sustain everyone—all living species and nature. It was heartening when, in 2017, New Zealand granted the Whanganui River the same legal rights as a person. The Whanganui became the first river in the world to be recognized as the living entity that rivers are, each with their own character.

Third, rivers—like power—defy simplistic measurement. With the Niger as our muse, we see that power is neither A nor B nor C, neither "power to" nor "power over" nor even "power with." Rather, simply, "power is." The Niger knows her kismet; she is not waiting for kindhearted humans to remove the obstacles that disrupt her labyrinthine journey toward self-actualization. Instead, she calmly keeps moving and revolts when necessary. This tells us that power is not something to feign but rather something to embody.

But perhaps most important, the branching of rivers teaches us that exousiance, the coming to power, is a complex *process*. At times the process is barely visible, like the gentle, lapping flow of a river surface while deep at the river's bottom a mighty stream surges. At other times a river's explosive movement is visible to the eye, for instance, when a dam can no longer withstand the force of the river dashing against it. However the movement happens, the river's motion is continuous. It is life and aliveness thrusting from within—the antidote to passive inaction. Power.

of BEAUTY

At some point in life the world's beauty becomes enough. You don't need to photograph, paint or even remember it. It is enough. No record of it needs to be kept and you don't need someone to share it with or tell it to. When that happens—that letting go—you let go because you can. The world will always be there—while you sleep it will be there—when you wake it will be there as well. So you can sleep and there is reason to wake.

—Toni Morrison, *Tar Baby*

To see beauty, is to be beauty

—Chris Abani, *The Face*

There can be no beauty in an oppressive system. Whatever is beautiful in a world shaped by Europatriarchal Knowledge is beautiful despite and not because of it. Whether it is a meadow defying environmental destruction or a peacock incandescently flaring its plumage or a woman feeling lovely and confident, everything genuinely beautiful exists in defiance of the oppressive framework that is Europatriarchy.

It's like the song "The Rose that Grew from Concrete," by rapper Tupac Shakur, where he speaks about a rose defying nature by growing from a crack in the pavement. Beauty in an oppressive system proves the system wrong; it stands in stark contrast to the ugliness of the social order.

Yet, beauty cannot be defined straightforwardly. Beauty is an enigma. Even the branch of philosophy that deals with beauty—aesthetics—has since its founding in the eighteenth century debated whether objects (people, things, nature) are in themselves beautiful or whether it is our projections of virtuous characteristics onto objects that make us perceive them as beautiful.

The belief that objects can be beautiful in themselves led predictably to formulaic attempts to measure precisely what then makes them beautiful. Is it their symmetry, proportion, or angles? William Hogarth, an eighteenth-century painter and critic, argued in his original but nonsensical book *The Analysis of Beauty* that beautiful objects possessed a "Line of Beauty." He called it a "serpentine line," which could be identified in the "female frame, represented in the Venus" and for which whiteness naturally became the yardstick. "As white is nearest to light," Hogarth wrote, "it may be said to be equal, if not superior, in value as to beauty."

In his 1933 book, *Aesthetic Measure*, mathematician George David Birkhoff made a similar argument. He argued that you can measure beauty with the formula $M = O/C$, where M is aesthetic measure, O is aesthetic order, and C is complexity. According to Birkhoff, the more order an object possesses, the higher its aesthetic standard.

Perhaps the best-known example of attempts to measure beauty is the application of the algebraic concept known as the golden ratio to the human face. The golden ratio, or the golden mean, stems from ancient Greece and is a ratio approximately equal to 1.618 that appears in nature, geometry, art, and architecture. But it was the German psychologist Gustav Theodor

Fechner who pioneered the idea that it could also be applied to the human face.

Those who believe that objects aren't necessarily beautiful in themselves argue that we perceive objects (people, things, nature) as beautiful only because we associate them with virtuous characteristics such as kindness, comfort, or elegance. In other words, beauty is in the eye of the beholder.

This notion of beauty—as connected to moral beliefs—is found across many cultures. The Yoruba word *ewa*, which means "beauty," forms the basis of the aesthetic concept *iwa l'ewa*, which connotes that good character and inner morality are synonymous with beauty. The Sanskrit concept *rasa*, defined by the Indian sage Bharata and later developed by the mystic and philosopher Abhinavagupta, describes beauty as a state of consciousness in which one experiences *visuddha-sattva*, freedom from egotism and cognitive emotions.

There are, of course, many other theories of beauty. For example, in his inimically sexist, yet otherwise hyperintelligent "Observations on the Feeling of the Beautiful and Sublime" the German philosopher Immanuel Kant argued that beauty is feminine, while sublimity is masculine (guess which was the superior quality?). There is also the idea that beauty is evolutionary, utilitarian, and instinctual. So peacocks developed their iridescent plumage to attract peahens; perky breasts are attractive because they symbolize youth, which in turn symbolizes fertility; red lips symbolize femininity; and so on. However, a growing number of scientists, most notably ornithologist Richard O. Prum, are disputing the idea that beauty is an outcome of adaptive evolution, arguing instead that animals—including humans—develop beauty just because it brings us pleasure.

Feminist contributions to the topic are mostly critical of beauty. Books such as critic Naomi Wolf's *The Beauty Myth* and political activist Sheila Jeffreys's *Beauty and Misogyny: Harmful Cultural Practices in the West*, although hardly reflecting a singular view on the topic, have criticized how beauty culture harms girls and women. There are books such as *Beauty Matters*, edited by philosopher Peg Zeglin Brand, and *Venus in the Dark*, by theorist Janell Hobson, which compellingly and invigoratingly investigate and revise beauty. But considering the significance of the topic in women's lives, there is little writing that tries to reconceptualize beauty with a feminist sensibility, and especially not with a black feminist one. Moreover, many critical ideas developed by feminists, such as the "male gaze," are insufficiently race conscious. It would be more appropriate to speak of a "Europatriarchal gaze," as men in many parts of the world have not traditionally idealized women first and foremost as sexual objects but, equally disturbingly as eternal mother figures or martyrs.

By contrast, in feminist art (fine art, photography, novels, music, and so forth) there is both a robust critique of beauty *as well as* a reconceptualization of beauty. I'm thinking of works such as *The Bluest Eye,* where Toni Morrison writes that beauty and the patriarchal construction of romantic love are "probably the most destructive ideas in the history of human thought. Both originated in envy, thrived in insecurity, and ended in disillusion." India Arie's *Acoustic Soul* is, you could argue, an album on how to grow Shakur's metaphorical rose from concrete. The paintings of artists such as Manuela Sambo, Mickalene Thomas, and Phoebe Boswell all critique and, most notably, reconfigure what beauty means.

The spirit of such works informs my goal in this book too, which is not merely to challenge our current understanding of beauty standards but to rethink them. In resisting manipulative Europatriarchal ideas, we tend to cynically condemn a concept that is in fact an essential tool with which to reimagine society. Beauty is too fecund an idea to give away. Beauty is not something women necessarily do for men, as is commonly assumed. Engaging with beauty is part of women's own history. For example, women have always used cosmetics for aesthetic enhancement but also for medicinal and ritualistic reasons. Ancient Egyptian women kept grounded galena stone—later called kohl—in small pots to apply around their eyes with a slim stick. Yoruba women still share this practice, only they call the grounded galena stones *tiiro* instead of kohl. In both cultures, applying galena around the eyes was not merely to enhance physical beauty; it was also to enhance health, as galena is believed to be antibacterial. Asian women used henna for similar purposes. Both African and Asian women removed body hair using copper razors dating back to 3000 BCE. Women in prisons today take high risks to acquire makeup and hair products, and—go figure—there are no men in women's prisons. There is a ritualistic element to beauty for women that has nothing to do with a male gaze but rather with self-care, as well as with female bonding.

It's no surprise that Europatriarchy corrupted the notion of beauty. If you want to control and manipulate women, get them to view beauty, an idea deeply embedded in their lives, as an inferior and competitive idea instead. That said, the convoluted connections between beauty, patriarchy, and capitalism mean that the relationship between feminism and beauty will always be contradictory. As bell hooks put it in *Feminism Is for Everybody*, "It has never been a simple matter for women to unite a love of beauty and style with comfort and ease." Still, even if the beauty industry is tied to Europatriarchy, beauty itself is a quality that we need more, not less, of in our lives.

To explore the myriad ways that beauty shapes our realities, I differentiate between three types of beauty narratives: Political Beauty, Artificial Beauty, and Genuine Beauty. In this chapter we look at these three types of beauty.

Political Beauty

Let us start, then, with the traditional source of Europatriarchal beauty ideals, the Bible. The Bible tells us that God created Adam, then provided him with a paradise garden containing animals, rivers, gemstones, abundant fruit, and Eve, a woman of divine perfection. She was gifted to Adam as a playmate. Eve exuded "sweet attractive Grace," wrote the poet John Milton in his magnum opus, *Paradise Lost*, painting a vivid word picture of her beauty: "Down to the slender waste [waist], / her unadorned golden tresses wore / Disheveld, but in wanton ringlets wav'd."

Across European history, distinguished artists such as Lucas Cranach the Elder, Hans Baldung, and Gustav Klimt continued to paint Eve's "sweet attractive grace" as though they used the same muse as their model—she who was made exclusively for Adam, with flowing golden tresses, fair skin, perky breasts, and an hourglass figure.

Eve's depiction in Genesis became the basis for the prevailing story of feminine beauty in the Western world, and Western ideals increasingly influenced the rest of the world. Today the image of beauty is slowly becoming more inclusive, with women of all backgrounds being portrayed as beautiful. Yet they qualify as beautiful on one condition only—they must adopt Eve as their role model. Regardless of a woman's heritage, to be considered beautiful by the mainstream, she must possess Eve-like attributes: the hourglass figure, the long flowing hair, ideally fair skin and European features, youthfulness, the seductive look in her eyes, the omnipresent approving gaze of Adam reflected in her every gesture.

Whether it is a nude Nastassja Kinski with a boa constrictor for *Vogue* or a naked Zoë Kravitz biting into the forbidden fruit in *Rolling Stone,* depictions of beauty in contemporary Western culture—striking as these are—remain unoriginal replicas of paintings of Eve by artists such as John Collier, Franz Stuck, or any of the artists mentioned above, if occasionally in blackface.

There is a common perception that beauty ideals change over time, but more than three thousand years after the myth of Adam and Eve was first recorded, not only do Eve's physical attributes still hold a grip on beauty ideals, the political agenda behind the Genesis story still thrives alongside. It is an agenda that connects male desire to power and female desire to submissiveness. It is, to put it differently, an agenda that makes oppression seem desirable for women. If only women can acquire beauty—or specific Euro-patriarchal ideals of feminine beauty—and therein the erotic desire it awakens in men, then they can access power. Whatever else women may achieve—ending wars or inventing cures to illnesses or leading thriving countries—pales in comparison to the sexual power they can amass through Eve-like beauty.

The political agenda of beauty not only seeks to eroticize women's oppression and to uphold specific attributes of white women as global standards of beauty, it also solidifies the idea that heterosexuality is the norm because it is only within a heteronormative culture that beauty can be used as a tool to oppress women. If heterosexual relationships and traditional gender roles were not privileged by the cultural and sociopolitical system, then the entire conceptualization of beauty would be turned on its head because beauty ideals would be disentangled from male desire and power. By *Political Beauty*, I therefore mean beauty ideals that serve primarily to boost a heteronormative Europatriarchal political agenda.

Political Beauty allows women one choice only, and that is whether to assess beauty as per the innocent version of Eve who, straight from Adam's rib, is righteous, sweet, and graceful, or whether to use the—infinitely more popular nowadays—beauty standards of Eve the seductive temptress, who recklessly condemned all of humanity to eternal suffering. The Eve dichotomy is presented to women as a choice, but it is merely an illusion of choice. Both Eves are centered on Adam's (or men's) desire of and access to power.

Consider, for example, the story of the German author Charlotte Roche, who in 2010 offered to have sex with then president of Germany, Christian Wulff, on the condition that he block legislation to extend the country's nuclear power stations. Despite the fact that Roche is a famous public intellectual in her own right, it was first of all her sex appeal (that is, closeness to Eve) that she used to access power. Her proposal is a perfect example of the Eve dichotomy. Was Roche sweet and righteous to selflessly offer her body as a sacrifice to save the world? Or was her tempting offer to save humanity from a disaster by providing her body instead subversive? We could debate the question endlessly, all the while missing the point, which is that the protagonist of this story is not Eve, it is Adam. Nobody knows (or cares) what Roche's motivations were because she, with her beauty, is just a supporting actor in the real story, which is male power-mongering. Examples like this, of which there are countless, and in which most of us are complicit to some extent show how invented connections (in this case biblical) between beauty, sexuality, heterosexuality, politics, and power can over time take the shape of a historical truth.

Of course, the Bible isn't the only source of patriarchy, misogyny, and heteronormativity. All religions are a form of institutionalized mythology, and in a patriarchal society, it is no surprise that mythology contributes to the oppression of women. That said, there are religions that afford women more power than Christianity (or Islam or Judaism, to include the leading beliefs). Women in Vedic culture, for instance, are historically able to access womanpower (*shakti*), and the most significant religious festival in South Asia, Diwali, is a celebration of *shakti* via the Hindu goddess Lakshmi, who as the goddess of wealth governs an auspiciously powerful domain. But one should tread carefully before claims that Hinduism, for example, provides an empowering and woman-centered faith. Lakshmi is, for instance, also the goddess of beauty, again connecting women's power to their physical appearance.

According to the Yoruba creation myth, the supreme deity Olodumare sent seventeen Orisha (gods), one of whom was a female goddess named Oshun, to populate the earth. But no sooner did the Orisha arrive on earth than did the sixteen male deities bully Oshun. She abandoned them and built herself a home in the forests.

Consequently, everything started to go wrong for the Orisha. They would build a house, and it would collapse. They would plant seeds, but a drought would follow. So they returned to Olodumare, who told them that the only way to fix the problem was to plead Oshun's forgiveness. When the deities found Oshun deep in the forest bathing in a still stream of a river, astonished by her resplendence, they bowed down and began to praise:

We will involve Oshun in all our deliberations
We are all on our knees

We are all begging you
Let us all kneel and prostrate before women
We are all born by women
Before we become recognized as human beings

Oshun accepted their apologies on two conditions. First, they must grant her a boy child, and second, women must be involved in every part of society apart from Egungun, the legendary masquerade for the ancestors.

In 2015 I visited the sacred grove of Oshun, where the goddess is to have made her abode. It was there that an Oshun priestess told me the creation myth I just shared. Although the myth gave a strong message of women's power, I was left wondering why Oshun insisted that her first child be male and why women can't participate in Egungun.

Also, if Olodumare believed a female deity was necessary for harmony, then why in god's name did they (the Yoruba god is gender neutral) only send one female and sixteen male Orisha to populate the earth in the first place? Additionally, like Eve and Lakshmi, Oshun is a goddess of beauty, implying once again that for a woman to be powerful, she must be beautiful. It seemed to me that this was a story not shaped by goddesses but by men.

Just as with the iconography of Eve in Genesis, Oshun's story is hardly neutral. It is drenched in a patriarchal political agenda. In fact, in today's climate it is increasingly conflated with biblical ideals of beauty. Search for goddess Oshun images on the web, for example, and a collage of Eve-in-blackface images will appear on your screen like a slot machine spewing out identically shiny coins. We need a retelling of Oshun that is absent of the Europa-triarchal gaze.

A few months after my visit to the Oshun grove, Beyoncé released her game-changing *Lemonade* album, with an accompanying video in which the star dresses up as Oshun or, to be more specific, as our contemporary, biblicized, Eve-like conception of Oshun. She is dressed in a flowing yellow Roberto Cavalli dress because Oshun's color is yellow. She is wearing golden jewelry because Oshun's element is gold. She appears underwater because Oshun's feature is water. And lo and behold, she also has tresses of disheveled golden waves down to her slender waist like, well, Eve.

To be clear, Beyoncé is not the issue here. Her image, like most women's, is entangled with the Political Beauty agenda. It is increasingly complicated to dissociate the politics from the agenda. Is it antifeminist to post revealing pictures on social media, or is it instead antifeminist that women's nipples are censored on social media platforms? It is also tricky to disentangle any penchant for beauty from the political agenda without seemingly reinforcing the agenda. Am I being a bad feminist if I wear lipstick? Or heels? Or thongs or waist beads? These are time-consuming questions that the agenda encourages us to debate rather than the real concern, which is that women are always trying to fit into a type created by men. If tomorrow men collectively decide that their ultimate woman is a dead woman, will women start killing themselves to fulfill male fantasies? Because that is what we do to our souls when we forever try to fit into the patriarchal mold of womanhood.

It is a mold that's always changing. One day men—themselves victims to the whims of patriarchal indoctrination—are convinced that beauty is women who have curves, only to change their minds the next day and prefer androgynous women. On Tuesday they like women in miniskirts, but come Saturday they prefer hijabs. At some times, they swoon over natural-looking women, but then they swing to the contoured, false-eyelashed, cosmetically altered look. Pubes one year, waxed pussy the next. Dress like a stripper one season, dress like a nun the next. They keep adding types too. The augmented reality type is growing in popularity, with her hybrid woman-robot look and body modifications. This could be exciting if led by a Sensuous Knowledge sensibility where aesthetics could be adventurous, eco-centric, and the like, rather than a Europatriarchal Knowledge one with its overemphasis on youth and mechanical aesthetic.

Throughout history and regardless of geography, men have held all kinds of preferences of the ideal woman but one—a woman with her own preferences. Men have used culture and tradition to construct feminine ideals, but they have never had the imagination or bravery to construct the archetype of a *woman*. A real human woman with her own psychological and sexual feelings. If women knew the confusion that men themselves feel about their inability to see women beyond a caricature, then maybe we would stop killing ourselves for a fickle system.

This is why Beyoncé's image is relevant, because it so perfectly conveys the continuing allure of the most popular construction of a type, Eve, even when blended with narratives from outside the West. Although Beyoncé is powerful in her own right and does not need to strengthen Europatriarchal beauty ideals to access power, she still chooses to. Ultimately, a choice itself tells us little. The complex and layered stories behind our decisions are what offer opportunities to make empowered choices.

When I visited the sacred groves of Oshun, I too wore a yellow dress, albeit (regrettably, on a freelance writer's salary) not a Cavalli. I wasn't much drawn to the mythology about Oshun—it was another Yoruba deity, Oya, goddess of transformation, who fascinated me at the time—but visiting Oshun's grove was indeed beautiful. The one-hundred-eighty-acre landscape is a place of phantasmagoric mystery. It is dotted with psychedelic sculptures, sanctuaries, and shrines that would have made surrealist artist Salvador Dali salivate. The grove's architecture is at once historical and futuristic, symbolic and straightforward, sinuous and symmetric. It's like walking through the subconscious, a place that feels utterly familiar yet totally mysterious at once. After a couple hours' walk, you eventually arrive at the pearl of the grove, the River Oshun. This is where the goddess is said to have bathed. And there she is, in the center of the meandering river, on a tiny island, as a mounted statue, bearing no resemblance to the mythical Eve whatsoever.

The Oshun grove does, however, coincidentally bear a resemblance to a piece of art, the beguiling *The Garden of Earthly Delights,* painted by the sixteenth-century Dutch artist Hieronymus Bosch.

Bosch's work is a triptych depicting three different worlds. On the left panel is the calm and serene garden of Eden, complete with the stereotypical representation of Eve. The center panel is a world of ecstatic curiosities, where humanity revels in a wild, psychedelic carnival of existence. Lastly, the right panel is a macabre world where iniquity has taken over, thanks to the revelry in the second panel. It is a fascinating art piece, not least because its conservative aim to dissuade people from pursuits of the senses is countered by its own sensuous play with hallucinatory symbolism.

It is the center panel in Bosch's triptych of which the Oshun grove reminds me. More specifically, it is the pool painted in the panel, in which a few dozen women are swimming, talking, and caressing, that is reminiscent of the River Oshun in the sacred grove. Like the river stream, Bosch's pool is surrounded by mysterious, distorted, anthropomorphic, and otherworldly figures, but the pool itself is an oasis of serenity.

In the corner of Bosch's pool, there is a black woman with a peacock (a symbol of beauty) on her head and a cherry (a symbol of sensuality) in her left hand. Bosch may not have known this, but the woman he painted is the goddess Oshun, whose spirit animal is indeed a peacock and who is the patron of sensuality.

The Garden of Earthly Delights was painted in the late sixteenth century—a period marked by the burgeoning transatlantic slave trade and by racist myths that were spun to legitimize it—so it is an astonishing place to encounter one of the earliest painted "Black Eves" in Western art history.

Or perhaps it isn't that surprising. The world of the West has, for a long time, tried to distort and demonize African womanhood. From historical art to modern-day icons such as Serena Williams, there's no doubt that a campaign to demean black beauty is ongoing and far-reaching. But Western history is also, if subtly, sprinkled with an appreciation of the beauty of African women, particularly dark-skinned African women.

While negative depictions of African women have always been dominant in the West, they have not been unchallenged. There has always been simultaneous awe of black women's ethereal beauty. The representations of black womanhood found in remnants of European arts such as the black Queen of Sheba or the shield of Kirchberg, which portrays a black female deity holding a lily stalk, are much more positive than would later be the case. As black at the time was the color of divinity, earth, and fertility, and women of dark hue from the ancient kingdoms such as Küsh, Meroë, and Nubia were queens and goddesses, it seems likely that these women were valued as especially beautiful and feminine.

Still, the portrayal of a black woman as an object of desire in sixteenth-century racist Europe is a pyrrhic victory if ever there were one. What we see in works such as Bosch's is the beginning of a special kind of racist and sexist process. The objectification of black women became tied not only to the eroticization of women's oppression but also to racial abuse. Then, as now, blackness was subject to atrocious discrimination in political and social life, but it was valued, objectified, and fetishized in cultural life.

When it comes to beauty, we need to detach our ideas of beauty from heteronormativity, patriarchy, and racism and re-define beauty from a woman-centered point of view. We need to explore beauty from an active rather than a passive position of womanhood—as subjects and not objects, as directors of the orchestra rather than the instruments to be played. The orchestra might look similar, but the song will sound different.

From such a position of active womanhood, it is Eve's rejection of authority that is bold and not Adam's cowardly projecting of his own wrongdoing onto her. Moreover, we might even question what Eve thought about Adam. Perhaps she was a lesbian and didn't think he was sexually attractive at all! Or, presuming Eve was attracted to men, then what was her response to Adam? Did she find him beautiful and desirable?

Nobody asks these questions because men are not judged by beauty. Women are beautiful and men are handsome. Tellingly, there is no political emphasis on handsomeness as there is on beauty. Europatriarchal artists, poets, and philosophers all have opinions about beauty, not handsomeness. Women are objects of beauty, and men analyze beauty. This has been the rule from ancient times until today. Conveniently, if the female body is seen as inherently more beautiful than the male, it is more "natural" to objectify it. Or so the circular Europatriarchal logic goes.

But what if women observed men as objects of beauty? What if we explored beauty rather than handsomeness in men? What would we discover if women politicized male beauty? Does the unclothed male body tell us anything about society? Can it convey the nature of human emotions such as vulnerability, strength, fear, boldness, seduction, and shyness? How does the male body age? And what do women artists make of the most expressive of body parts, the penis, when it's not viewed as a phallic object with larger-than-life superpowers?

Some years ago, in an attempt to respond to these questions, I launched an Instagram account with the handle @maleobjects and the description "An exploration of men and beauty." I hoped that the page would help me answer the questions that nagged at me about men and beauty. They were questions that went beyond attraction, or lust, into the domains of what we could call the "deeply political" and the "deeply personal," which of course were intertwined. Alas, my time for this project was limited and the posts infrequent, but the project stayed in the back of my mind, and every so often I returned to it.

The first lesson I learned was that images of male beauty are hard to come by. I came across many homoerotic photos, but they had a different purpose than my woman-centered, black-woman-gaze aims. Of course, the internet is full of photographs of incredibly handsome men, but I was after images of men that engaged with beauty, not handsomeness. I therefore also wasn't interested in images of men from mainstream popular culture—stereotypical images of handsome and heroic masculinity such as Erik Killmonger in *Black Panther* or suave villains like James Bond. Even the "soft" sensitive Ryan Gosling types created for a female audience were banned from @maleobjects for their predictability.

It was not surprising that images of male beauty were hard to find. Not only was there a time when women were banned from the art world at large, but there is also a stigma of aggression and vulgarity attached to women's engagement with the male body and a hypocritical taboo surrounding the depiction of male genitals. As the artist Nicole Wittenberg, who paints beguiling male nudes, says, "A dick painting may be the most impossible thing to sell, ever." Yet as the Fight Censorship Group, a women's arts organizations said, "If the erect penis is not wholesome enough to go into museums, it should not be considered wholesome enough to go into women."

The second thing I discovered was that to post images of male beauty, I needed to explore which qualities make a man beautiful, a task that is neither objective nor straightforward. The project made me reflect on the period of time when I started to become aware of myself as a sexual being. I read old journal entries of mine about the boys in my class transforming from children into young men when we returned to school from a summer holiday. I learned that I have always behaved in that sexually free way that men do—in my head, of course. I was enthralled by their deepened voices, by spurts in their height, by their bulging Adam's apples as well as bulges in their pants. I remembered a classmate's testicles being visible through the hem of his shorts, and later that evening allowing my fingers to journey under my underwear to dance with body parts I did not yet know how to describe. You could say I had a sort of penis envy in knowing that expressing my desires as a woman would never be seen with the agency that they would be seen with if I were male.

My aim was thus not to create an account that would speak to everyone's definitions of male beauty, although I did plan to explore the female gaze through other female artists' interpretations, so it was collaborative in that regard. The features that I attributed to male beauty were normative and subjective. As mentioned, we may think of the terms *beautiful* and *handsome* as equal, but although they certainly overlap, they are significantly different because handsomeness, unlike beauty, has no political charge.

And so I came to conceive of male *beauty* as an unrehearsed type of manliness, a kind of natural poise that didn't appear to be trying to be manly in the dogmatic and stoically macho way we define manliness. The images that I selected were marked by movement and sensuality. They conveyed strength—not in a strictly physical sense but rather in the sense of being energetic, passionate, and playful while simultaneously tender and open. I was interested in how the male body blends into its environment; how lithe limbs could seem at one with the branches of a tree; how male hands appear against the black-blue color of the night; how men look wading through rivers like graceful mermaids. There was a quality of contemplation to the images I selected (from an already limited pool, and after Instagram repeatedly deleted my posts—a deleting that was even more annoying when it came to black men as it was especially difficult to find portrayals of black men with the unrehearsed manliness I refer to). I became primarily intrigued with images that conveyed a man seemingly contemplating what freedom may look like from a male perspective.

To my disappointment, my third realization was that with the exception of artists such as Sylvia Sleigh and Leonor Fini, relatively few women had objectified men, let alone the male body. Whether in fine art, photography, scripture, or sculpture, we are historically deprived of female interpretations of her male counterpart. However, things are slowly changing; a growing number of artists, such as Celia Hempton and Lynette Yiadom-Boakye, are interpreting men in captivating ways.

The novelist and poet John Berger famously wrote in his extraordinary book *Ways of Seeing* that in most imagery, "Men act and women appear. Men look at women. Women watch themselves being looked at." I discovered how true this still is. In addition, women too look at women. Men are preoccupied with defining female beauty, and women also are preoccupied with feminine beauty. Female artists are more likely to paint women than men. There is nothing wrong in women painting women, of course. But there is a conspicuous absence of women objectifying men.

Objectifying the male body is not about vengeance, nor is it strictly about titillation. Many of the images I posted did not evoke sexual desire as much as they invoked the thirst for balance. There was thus an underlying sentiment of restoration in my posting.

In the New Testament book of 1 Timothy it says, "A woman should learn in quietness and full submission. I do not permit a woman to teach or to have authority over a man; she must be quiet (1 Tim. 2: 11-12)." I was motivated to counter the "loud" female quietness when it comes to objectifying the male body. For as the Zimbabwean author Yvonne Vera said in "Opening Spaces: An Anthology of Contemporary African Women's Writing," "I am against silence."

Artificial Beauty

A Zairean proverb asks, The teeth are smiling, but is the heart? In 2016, while in Jamaica to give a public lecture about African feminism, I visited a restaurant up in the Blue Mountains that brought this saying to mind.

The dreamy venue was accentuated by a strikingly beautiful waiter—tall and chiseled, with thick, coily hair that surrounded his head like a helmet—who carried himself with a regal poise that I came to associate with Jamaicans. His only aesthetic flaw was that he had bleached his skin so much that his epidermis looked as delicate as a thin film of egg white. It hurt my eyes to look at his sore skin, but at the same time I could not take them off him; his striking looks and put-on accent attracted my attention. I wanted to understand why he was trying so hard to portray himself as something other than who he perceived himself to be. What makes a person voluntarily rub harmful chemicals into their skin to achieve a lighter skin tone?

I thought of the work of two scholars whose contrasting arguments about skin bleaching I was familiar with. American-Ghanaian scholar Dr. Yaba Blay argues that people bleach their skin as a "consequence of global White supremacy." And Nigerian scholar Dr. Bibi Bakare-Yusuf, in contrast, argues that skin bleaching is not necessarily a reflection of a desire to be white but rather "a superficial form of self-styling, a form of adornment and bodily enhancement, just like plastic surgery, make-up or hair straightening." I had always wished to bring these two viewpoints into a conversation and to mull over how they were entangled with class, sexuality, and gender. The waiter provided a reference point.

If my waiter was of the view, however unconsciously, that whiteness "has been promoted as the essence of being human, civilised, beautiful and superior . . . while Blackness has been associated with being bestial, barbaric, ugly and inferior," as Blay argues, then his bleaching may have had to do with self-loathing, with a sense of dissatisfaction with himself because of an internalized racism and colorism.

If, by contrast, as Bakare-Yusuf argues, lightening the skin is not always "about devaluing blackness" but rather "about expressing one's participation in the global fashion system, and showing off an ability to rework socio-biological memes," then perhaps he used skin color modification to express a belonging to a global, urbane, cosmopolitan, middle-class community. Probably his bleaching was aspirational rather than self-deprecating. As Bakare-Yusuf goes on to say, "There is no shame or hatred or deep reflection behind the choice. It is a fashion statement, a way to show-off and be the subject of marvel."

Bakare-Yusuf's point seemed apt; the waiter did not convey a desire to be white. Given what little I knew about him—that he worked in a boutique hotel visited by middle- and upper-class locals and tourists, that he was attractive and seemed aware of it, that he was jovial and well spoken and proud of his Jamaican heritage—I mused that perhaps he bleached his skin to come across as worldly and to add an air of sophistication to his self-presentation.

Yet of course, notions of worldliness are interwoven with qualities of whiteness. Worldliness is, after all, associated with material comforts, and whiteness is, globally speaking, a signifier of material comfort and class privilege. This measure of whiteness as worldly is, I believe, the basis of subservient behavior by black people toward white people rather than because of their race per se. I have observed how working class Nigerians will for example be standoffish toward a white person whom they've gleaned isn't wealthy. And their deferential treatment toward white wealthy people is no different from their behaviour toward wealthy black people. It is often the result of wealth that is inscribed in whiteness that causes subservience in black people rather than any sense of racial inferiority. In this regard, Blay's argument that skin bleaching and racism are tied together remains indisputable.

Worldliness is also connected to beauty, insofar as a kind of globally unidentifiable appearance can be tied to beauty. People who look as though they could come from virtually anywhere—

mostly Latin Americans, Mediterraneans, North Africans, the Roma, and Indians—are regularly ascribed beauty on that basis alone. As Bakare-Yusuf writes about Lagosian women who bleach, they want people to attest "to the fact that the flashing, mascaraed eyes are speaking Latin, the shimmering red lips are talking Spanish and the hydroquinoned skin is radiating beauty."

The notion of worldliness informs colorism also. In the instances when my light skin is fetishized, it is clear that the person doing the fetishizing attributes to me not only an aesthetic judgment rooted in white supremacy but also a projection of class-privileged worldly status, and the many problematic and complex layers of desire and disconnection embedded in such a status. In my local grocery store in Lagos, one of the staff once told me that he wished he had my skin color, and when I asked him why he simply responded, "It will be nice to be yellow like you." There was no desire to possess my actual skin tone in his remark, and certainly not whiteness. What he desired were the privileges he perceived that I must have because of my skin color. My "yellow-ness" represented an economic opportunity, not beauty.

Bakare-Yusuf's essay is titled "Yellow Fever Nko" (Pidgin English for "What About Yellow Fever?"), and Blay's essay is called "On Yellow Fever." Both articles are in conversation with the 1976 hit song by Fela Kuti titled "Yellow Fever," in which he gave mass appeal to the use of the term *yellow* to describe light skin. The frenzy to want light "yellow" skin was, according to Fela, comparable to other fevers such as "malaria fever," "jaundice fever," and "influenza fever."

Yellowness is an apt reference point also for a discussion about Artificial Beauty because yellow is the color that the eye notices first. This is why signposts are yellow. It is why so many flowers have yellow petals—so that they can attract pollinators. We consider things that are yellow beautiful simply because we notice yellow things easily. But just because something is easily noticed does not mean it is pleasant to see. Many dangerous and poisonous animals are also yellow to warn others from getting near. Yellow is also the color of jaundice, which can signify a severe illness. The need to be noticed is mostly about a need to encourage attention to something else, and in the case of Artificial Beauty, that "something else" is the expedition of capital. Whether it is financial capital, social capital, or cultural capital, Artificial Beauty draws attention to itself so that others will expend some form of capital on acquiring it.

When it comes to women, Artificial Beauty charges the rent for the existing Political Beauty construction. It cajoles women into thinking that if only they expend capital on this, that, or the other, they will grow closer to the Eve image, and the closer to the Eve image they get, the happier and the more successful they will become. But no sooner has the female consumer expended capital on the promise of Eve-ian beauty (and subsequent access to male desire and power) than she realizes that it was a trick, a filter, a savvy advertising ploy, a skilled surgeon, you name it, and not the peace of mind that she hoped for. Artificial Beauty has no substance. Beneath its veneer it is empty.

The point is not that beauty cannot be reflected in exterior looks. Looking one's best and feeling one's best often go hand in hand. People who have "beauty privilege" may find it easier to look their best, but as with all privilege, it can have the effect of blinding you to reality, and perceiving reality is the basis of joy.

Note too that all objects are in some sense artificial. Nothing is ever quite what we perceive it to be. Having historical value doesn't automatically make a thing better than something quickly patched together in a Chinese factory. Rejecting Artificial Beauty does not mean abstaining from beauty entirely; it means seeing the lie behind the beauty narrative. To see the lie is to disempower it.

Nor is the point to reject desirability altogether. Everybody likes to be considered desirable, especially by someone they themselves want, but there is a big difference between being desired for your individuality—your unique look, voice, smell, thoughts, laugh, and so forth—and being desired because you have the attributes that a manufacturer of narrative somewhere, sometime, decided would help sell their products, be that product a physical object or a racist worldview.

In 2016 I hosted a conversation with the legendary feminist activist and author Nawal El Saadawi at the Waterstones bookshop in Piccadilly in London, which crystallized some of these questions. After the talk, at dinner, I felt a camaraderie with Nawal that I might best describe as "girly," in the most positive meaning of the adjective. Gone was my nervousness about meeting someone whom I admired so much, and instead we drank gin and tonics (both our favorite drink) and debated topical issues with the rest of the company. Suddenly Nawal turned to me and said in her refreshingly straightforward and critically thinking way, "You know your tattoos are patriarchal, don't you?"

Her remark caught me off guard. I understood tattoos on women as many things, but it never occurred to me to think of them as patriarchal. To the contrary, having been a tattooed woman since I was a teenager—that is, since long before it was fashionable and widely acceptable for women to be tattooed—I'd often felt that, if anything, men reacted judgmentally to my tattoos. But she had a point. Tattoos attract attention to the body.

Already as a child, I dressed my favorite Barbie—the one that represented my inner self (if I may be Freudian)—in black from head to toe and drew tattoos on her. My preferred look for her was not stereotypically feminine or Eve-like. I cut her long black hair short and painted pointy cat eyes on her. My childhood play was symbolic of a cultural upbringing where beauty standards were rigid and beauty was centralized in my impressionable brain, but my restyling of the doll was also emblematic of resistance to that cultural upbringing. It was patriarchal socialization *and* protofeminist resistance in one.

My relationship with makeup is still a reflection of this contradictory relationship. I own more makeup than is reasonable, especially as a relatively light makeup wearer. Not only do I spend money on products I barely end up using, but I also spend more time than I'd like to admit choosing those products I do use—which mascara curls best or what concealer is best for dark circles or which powder is the most matte. In fairness, I also spend an objectionable amount of time deciding which ink cartridges or coffee makers to buy, so my makeup shopping is symptomatic of being a modern consumer with an exhausting amount of products to choose from. My relationship to makeup is, however, informed by socialized ideas of female beauty as well as by consumerism. I'm by no means absolved of this world, but I also love makeup for the reasons many women always have; it is ritualistic and it also connects me to a lineage of female bonding through art and expression.

Nawal's question brought the realization of yet another contradiction. My appreciation of tattoos has to do with the idea of the body as a canvas. This is quite a modern and Western interpretation of tattooing. Historically, tattoos had to do with belonging and community. In the West they were seen, as the 1902 *Century Dictionary* describes it, as "something to be found on uncivilised people," which is hilarious when you consider that most tattooed people today are Westerners. But that is also what drew me to tattooing—that at the time it was anti-Europatriarchal for a woman to ink her body permanently.

Women can't possibly always make the best choices in societies so full of incompatible myths about femininity. What we can strive to do is cultivate a mind at rest and ease regardless of the fleeting events in life, which is necessary for making empowering choices. Feminism ought to focus more on providing tools that bring clarity. Bleaching your skin does not make you worldly, dark skin has a history we are discouraged to appreciate to uphold colorism, makeup does not make you feminine, and tattoos do not in themselves protect you from the male gaze. The halo around the moon is not the moon, and so too the specter of beauty is not beauty itself. It is merely a simulacrum of it, an artificial distillation of the sparkle that is genuine beauty.

Genuine Beauty

How could our ancestor of long ago paint so delicately? How could a brute who fought wild beasts with his bare hands create images so filled with grace? How did he manage to draw those flying lines that break free of the stone and take to the air? How could he? ...

Or was it she?

—Eduardo Galeano, *Mirrors*

Beauty is not democratic, or it would cease to be beauty. Even when people are manipulated to hold the same beauty standards, they *still* have preferences for a particular look, specific architecture, certain colors, certain environments, certain music, individual books. Beauty is anarchic, if anything. It is not a question of general consensus but rather an expression of rebelling against conformity. This sense of personal experience forms part of reenvisioning our relationship to beauty.

For this reason, beauty is also a cultural experience. Roundness is seen as beautiful in many parts of Africa; in some Mauritanian and Moroccan communities, they even practice *leblouh*, which involves force-feeding women ahead of marriage. Similar practices are found among the Efik in Nigeria, who historically placed young women eligible for marriage in *nkuhos*, or fattening rooms. Maori women adorn their chins with *tā moko*, a traditional tattoo with a sacred meaning. In Tajikistan, unibrows are considered beautiful, while women in medieval England would pluck their eyebrows and hairlines to give the appearance of a high forehead. The Mende in Sierra Leone considered a smooth, tall, and shiny black forehead to be beautiful. The Akan of Ghana also find a big forehead attractive as they take it to symbolize knowledge. To the Yoruba spread across Nigeria, Benin, and Togo, a gap between the upper front teeth is a mark of beauty. In an interview I watched recently with a Maasai man adorned in elaborate jewelry, the reporter asks, "Both women and men can wear these?" He looks at her as though she had asked him if both women and men can eat. "Yes, it's just for beauty and decoration," he replies self-evidently. Fela Kuti's wives, or queens as he called them, created beauty ideals that had nothing to do with Eve. They had smooth and porcelain dark skin, gap teeth, sinuous bodies, power, sensuality, sass. Cultural beauty ideals open our minds to the malleability of beauty, yet these practices too are entwined with patriarchy and elitism. The *tā moko* mentioned above is a signifier of status; Fela's queens, while seeming mostly content, had to share one man among twenty-seven of them, which is a big compromise at least sexually if not romantically; and the *leblouh* is, needless to say, abusive to girls and women.

The experience of beauty is also secretive. As children, we are susceptible to the forms of beauty discussed here—the Political Beauty in our favorite Disney princess movie or the Artificial Beauty of our Barbie dolls. But we are also subject to Genuine Beauty. When we play outdoors or paint or even just conjure a fantasy world in our minds, as children we are always cultivating our own culture, our own understanding of beauty. It is this childlike quality of defining beauty for oneself, almost like having a personal secret, rather than defining it by way of socially constructed stimulants, that awakens our dulled senses and brings us closer to Genuine Beauty.

More than anything, we wake up when we see the ugliness that we are meant to think of as beauty—the classism, racism, colorism, sexism, repression, bleaching, conformity to one image of Eve. How did we come to see this as beautiful?

Genuine Beauty has to do with the eternal. If beauty were a garden, then Political Beauty would be a garden where all plants were organized into identical pots. Artificial Beauty would be an illusory garden. Once you stepped into it, you would realize it was merely a projection. You would try to pluck a flower, but there would be nothing there. You would not see your reflection in the garden's ponds because all would be a simulation. You would bite into ripe fruit and realize that it has no taste. If Genuine Beauty were a garden it would be one where each blade of grass, each solitary leaf, and even the tiniest petals sparkle in their unique glory, as they have done since the beginning of time.

Toni Morrison wrote in *The Bluest Eye*, "Beauty was not simply something to behold; it was something one could *do*." Do beauty, dear reader. Do beauty like your life depends on it, because in many ways it does. All our lives do. Beauty in action is art, and the more we strive to make of life an art, the more beautiful our world and we ourselves will become. I have never seen a person, no matter what age, look, ability, height, this or that, be passionate about life and not be beautiful.

Sight. Hearing. Taste. Smell. Touch. The word *beauty* stems from the Latin *bellitatem*, which means "a state of being pleasing to the senses." Each of the five senses is a sensor for beauty. We have at least twenty-one senses, writes genealogist Bruce Durie in the *New Scientist* in "Senses Special: Doors of Perception," including equilibrioception, a sense of balance, and chronoception, a sense of time. How do these additional senses help "do beauty"?

As Yvonne Vera said in an interview with Jean Bryce published in *Sign and Taboo*, "I would not write if I weren't in search of beauty, if I was doing it only to advance a cause." Vera's words come to mind as this book approaches its end. For although there are a number of causes that I have wished to advance, it is my hope that it has not been at the cost of beauty.

In my garden in Lagos grow bushes of a plant called *Costus spectabilis*, also known as the yellow trumpet, also known as the national flower of Nigeria. Its yellow flowers open from the stamen of the flower into a gathering of petals formed into a flared bell. They look like trumpets, but they make me think of ears, because every morning the leaves open like ears to listen to the world. And every night the buds of my Co-Spec, as I call her, close inward like a clenched fist—an act that makes me think of resistance. It's as though the "ears" have heard enough of our ways for the day. Yet come morning, they resign their objection. They forgive our betrayals and in so doing are themselves absolved from the crime of unhearing.

Throughout this book, I have tried to be like the yellow

trumpet, listening to what needed to be heard, and closing my ears to that which no longer is useful. Still, every morning, as I resumed writing, it was with the willingness to listen more and dig deeper. Yet as the book comes to a close, I am all too aware of everything I didn't hear and therefore didn't say.

So I'll close the book where it began, with the story of "The Mountain," where two explorers saw the mountain differently depending on their perspective. Can I suggest that there is yet a perspective that is neglected in our collective consciousness? It is the position of the mountain itself. The mountain sees the art of life, the tremor of life, the ideas of life, the seasons of life. And can I suggest that what the mountain above all perceives—witness as it is to the two explorers and to everything that surrounds them—is beauty?

ACKNOWLEDGMENTS

While I alone am responsible for the contents of this book, I want to express my gratitude to those who directly or indirectly enabled my writing it. Above all, thank you, mum, for nurturing your vision through me. I'm your imperfect but unique work of art, and there's nothing I'd rather be. Thank you, dad, your wit, wisdom and graciousness were an inspiration to me while writing this book, as they always are. Thank you, aunties, uncles, cousins, extended family in Malmö, Lagos, Finland and beyond, for your unhesitating support of this book, and of me. Thank you, cherished friends, you know who you are, for being patient and supportive while I was in solitary book-writing mode, but equally ready to indulge in cathartic reflection and good times when I craved a break. Thank you, writers and poets, for the motivating companionship of your words. Thank you, feminists, for the long tradition of envisioning new worlds and resisting old ones. Thank you, Earth, for nurturing and providing space to cultivate creative expression. Thank you, Maria Cardona Serra, for being a supportive and reassuring, but also a firm and focused agent. You, and the Pontas agency, have been amazing. Thank you, Zed and Amistad/

Harper Collins, and my editors Kim Walker and Tracy Sherrod for believing in me and helping to bring the best possible version of *Sensuous Knowledge* into the world. Last but certainly not least, thank you readers of MsAfropolitan, for being readers of MsAfropolitan! This book would not exist if not for the true gift it has been to grow and share this journey with you.

Olokun fẹ mi lo'rẹ, mo dupe.

RECOMMENDED READING

For further resources related to Sensuous Knowledge including book recommendations, artists, scholars, musicians, inspirations, organisations, poets, healers and dreamers, please visit: www.msafropolitan.com/sensuous-knowledge.

ABOUT THE AUTHOR

MINNA SALAMI is a Nigerian, Finnish, and Swedish author, blogger, and social critic and an international keynote speaker. She is the founder of the multiple award-winning blog *MsAfropolitan*, which connects feminism with critical reflections on contemporary culture from an Africa-centered perspective. Listed by *Elle* magazine as "one of twelve women changing the world" alongside Angelina Jolie and Michelle Obama, Minna has presented talks on feminism, liberation, decolonization, sexuality, African studies, and popular culture to audiences at the European Parliament, the Oxford Union, Yale University, TEDx, the Singularity University at NASA, and UN Women. She is a contributor to *The Guardian, Al Jazeera,* and the Royal Society of the Arts and is a columnist for the *Guardian Nigeria*. She lives in London.